ONE·OF·A·KIND

Handmade
WEDDINGS

LAURA MAFFEO & COLLEEN MULLANEY

Creative Publishing
international

Creative Publishing
international

First published in the United States of America by Creative Publishing international, Inc., a member of

Quayside Publishing Group
400 First Avenue North
Suite 300
Minneapolis, MN 55401
1-800-328-3895
www.creativepub.com

ISBN-13: 978-1-58923-610-3
ISBN-10: 1-58923-610-6

10 9 8 7 6 5 4 3

Library of Congress Cataloging-in-Publication Data

Maffeo, Laura.
  One-of-a-kind weddings. Invitations and paper details / Laura Maffeo, Colleen Mullaney.
    p. cm. -- (One-of-a-kind weddings)
  ISBN 978-1-58923-610-3
1. Paper work. 2. Weddings--Equipment and supplies. I. Mullaney, Colleen, 1966- II. Title. III. Series.

  TT870.M22 2009
  745.54--dc22

2008022239

Cover and Book Design: Sandra Salamony
Page Layout: Sandra Salamony
Photographs: Jack Deutsch Photography
Copy Editor: Carol Polakowski
Proofreader: Julia Maranan

Printed in China

CONTENTS

PART I   INVITATIONS & PAPER DETAIL

PART II   FAUX FLORALS & CANDLES

PART I
INVITATIONS & PAPER DETAILS

Every bride wants her wedding to be a one-of-a-kind event. She looks for details and personal touches that reflect her style and the style of her groom. Paper plays such an important role in a wedding—from the invitations to the program and written vows—that it's the perfect material to work with to customize your day.

Whether you're planning the place cards or the cocktail napkins, the guestbook or the décor, the unique personality of the happy couple will shine through in each of the details. Paper embellishments can be showcased in decorations on walls and tables, favors, and save-the-date cards—and everything in between. No small element should be overlooked.

Paper is versatile and easy to work with and can be cost-efficient, too. A few, well-chosen extra details can change a wedding from an ordinary affair to a truly inspired event—without breaking even the most thrifty bride's budget. Here are some ideas for working with paper to help you showcase your own personal flair, to make your wedding a one-of-a-kind day that no one will ever forget.

CHAPTER 1

SAVE-THE-DATES AND ANNOUNCEMENTS

Save-the-date cards and announcements are the first steps you take when planning your wedding. These important pieces of paper tell the world who you are, whom you love, and what you hope your future holds. They also set the theme and tone for the rest of your wedding events, so why not add a bit of your own individuality and style? Whether you prefer a sparkly shadowbox announcement or a sweet and simple bookmark, these projects will help you find your own special way to express your joy and excitement as you spread the word about the amazing day ahead!

SHADOWBOX ANNOUNCEMENT

Wedding announcements should be fun and original. They announce to the world the joining of two people in love! With this unique shadowbox, you can spread the good news to your loved ones in style. The materials are easy to find, and the technique is simple and quick. Mix up your design by choosing bright silver stars or colorful confetti. Choose colors and papers that reflect your wedding theme, coordinated with your other paper details. These announcements are as much fun to make as they are to receive.

Here are the materials you will need to make one shadowbox announcement:

- one 5" × 7" (12.5 × 18 cm) paper photo card with 2 ¹/₂" × 4" (6.5 × 10 cm) window opening
- one plastic sheet protector
- paper in color of your choice, for announcement
- one large, decorative rubber stamp
- one rubber-stamp ink pad
- clear double-sided tape
- foam double-sided tape
- small plastic confetti
- scissors

STEP 1.   Cut apart the photo card. Discard the middle piece of paper (you'll use only the front and back of the card).

STEP 2.   Cut the sheet protector in half. Cut it in half again to make a total of eight small plastic sheets, measuring 4" × 5 1/4" (10 × 13.5 cm).

STEP 3.   Working with the decorative rubber stamp and ink pad, stamp two opposite corners on the front of the top photo card. Try to place each design motif in the same position on each corner—but you don't have to be exact.

STEP 4.   Adhere the plastic sheet onto the inside of the top photo card with the clear double-sided tape.

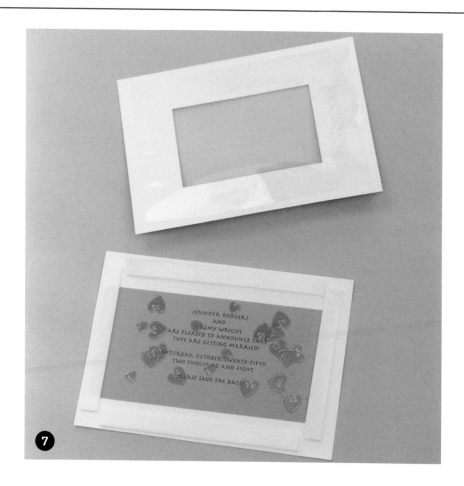

STEP 5.   Print your announcement on the colored paper—by hand or with
a computer and color printer (we used a 14-point font in our word
processing program). Position the announcement so you can cut
the paper to a size of 4" × 6" (10 × 15 cm).

STEP 6.   Attach the announcement to the center front of the bottom photo
card with clear double-sided tape. Make sure the announcement is
centered in the window of the card before securing it.

STEP 7.   Frame the front outside edge of the bottom photo card with foam
double-sided tape. Sprinkle a small amount of plastic confetti inside
the foam-tape frame. Place the top window frame onto the bottom
card, making sure it sits evenly on all sides.

SAVE-THE-DATE BOOKMARK

Of course, a bride wants to make sure no one misses her big day. Before sending out your invitations, secure the date with friends and family by sending them this cheery save-the-date bookmark. This little reminder will not only keep their place in the books they're reading, but it will also help them keep their schedules clear. Provide all the information on where and when or just print up the date and a simple phrase or poem. Your loved ones will be thinking of you from one chapter to the next!

Here are the materials you will need to make two save-the-date bookmarks:

- one 4 $1/2$" × 6 $1/4$" (11.5 × 16 cm) card, yellow
- one 5" × 7" (12.5 × 18 cm) card, orange
- scissors
- craft glue
- single-hole punch
- 12" (30.5 cm) length of $1/2$" (1.3 cm)-wide ribbon

STEP 1. Print your save-the-date information on the yellow card with a color printer. You can print two bookmarks on one card by formatting the document into two columns and duplicating the information. Make sure the text is centered within both columns.

STEP 2. Cut both cards in half lengthwise.

STEP 3. Center one small card on top of one large card and glue together. Allow the glue to dry.

Mark it
in
the books!

SANDRA FOSTER
and
KEVIN MARSHALL

Are

Getting

Married!

Saturday

June 6,

2009

In Vero Beach,
Florida!

We hope
To see
You
There!

STEP 4.   Punch a hole ³/₄" (2 cm) from the bottom of the bookmark.

STEP 5.   Fold the ribbon in half and feed both ends through the back of the hole.

STEP 6.   Pull ends through the loop gently to secure the ribbon to the bookmark.

Nell and Tom are Getting Married
Please save the date
November 8th 2008

SAVE-THE-DATE DÉCOUPAGE VOTIVE

Everyone loves to find a surprise in the mailbox. Here's a sweet and sendable trinket to announce your wedding day. These votives will fit easily into small mailing tubes. Remember to check the postage of each votive before mailing. This project is not only a terrific gift to receive but is also fun to make. Gather your girlfriends together, serve some cocktails and snacks, and have yourself a découpage craft night. Choose scented candles for an extra sensory surprise!

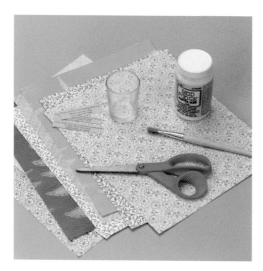

Here are the materials you will need to make one save-the-date découpage votive:

- paper, in color of your choice, for announcement
- assorted scrapbooking papers or other decorative papers
- scissors
- small glass votive
- découpage glue
- small paintbrush

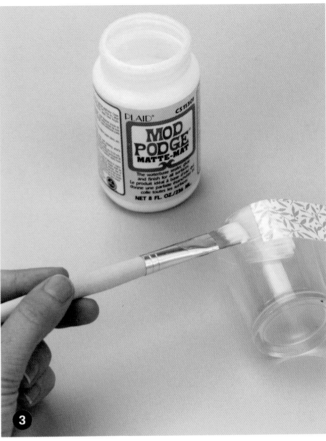

STEP 1.   Print your save-the-date information onto colored paper with
a computer.

STEP 2.   Cut assorted colors of paper into different-size strips, all ½" (1.3 cm)
wide and ranging from 1" to 3" (2.5 to 7.5 cm) in length.

STEP 3.   Paint a layer of the découpage glue onto a small area of the votive.

STEP 4.   Stick a strip of decorative paper onto the glue. Paint more glue onto
the strip of paper until it is saturated.

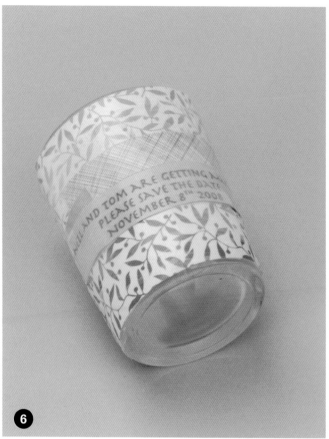

STEP 5.   Continue gluing strips of paper, alternating sizes, onto the votive, overlapping the strips slightly.

STEP 6.   After you have covered the entire votive with decorative paper strips, place the strip of paper with the save-the-date information on the center of the votive and cover with glue.

STEP 7.   Paint a final layer of glue over the entire votive, making sure all the paper is saturated. Let the découpage dry overnight before packaging it up to send.

More Ideas

VINTAGE AND SPECIALTY POSTCARDS

Vintage postcards have loads of character. They take us back to the glamorous long-ago days of adventure and travel. Print your save-the-date information onto a small mailing label and stick it right onto the back of these small time capsules.

You can easily find vintage postcards in antique stores, flea markets, and online. Or you can print your own vintage postcards with your computer and printer (you'll find cards and templates at most office supplies stores and online). You'll personalize your wedding, while also recycling charming forgotten treasures from the past.

MAGNETIC PHOTO SAVE-THE-DATE

The refrigerator door is a favorite place to display reminders—from dentist appointment postcards to lists of things to do. Why not tidy things up by sending a save-the-date that won't compete for door space? Here's a way to ensure guests will remember your day each time they check their grocery lists.

Print up a cute photo and a little information about your wedding in the format of a business card (most word-processing programs provide this option). Simply stick the card onto business-card-size magnets that have adhesive on the back (sold at most office supplies stores). If you don't have time to do the printing, office supplies stores will do that part for you, at minimal cost. Keep it simple or add a decorative border.

IN-THE-MOOD CD ANNOUNCEMENT

Here's a great way to get your friends and family in the mood. Create a mix CD of all your favorite songs—to remind them of the date and get them ready to celebrate.

Choose songs that suit your wedding location (leave your heart in San Francisco?) or have the party mood you want to recreate (Jamaican reggae, anyone?). Customize the CD sticker to suit the style or place. (You'll find CD sticker kits at most office supplies stores.) Best of all, you'll give your guests a gift they can enjoy long after the day is done.

CALENDAR STICKER REMINDER

All of us struggle to keep our schedules straight. These simple, smart calendar stickers are a great way to remind your friends and family that a big day is coming. Enclose them with your save-the-date cards or wedding announcements. Guests can stick them into their day-planners, on a calendar page, or on the refrigerator.

You can make them in just minutes on your home printer. Labels come in all sorts of shapes, colors, and sizes (make sure to choose one that is compatible with your printer). Select a design that jumps off the page or something simple that gets the job done. Either way, your guests will start to plan their days around your special event.

Please Join Us for a
Bridal Brunch
Celebrating

Jennifer Lewis

Saturday, March 7th
At 12 pm

Hosted by
Laura Willis
123 Juniper Rd.
White Plains, NY
914.555.7865

CHAPTER 2

INVITATIONS

Invitations are the cornerstones of your wedding. They launch the event and set the tone. They can be traditional and elegant or modern and bold—as simple or as sophisticated as the bride herself. Regardless of whether your event is a fun bridal shower or a black-tie affair, your invitations should delight and intrigue your guests.

When you add a dash of your personal style to your invitation design, you let those nearest and dearest to you know that everything about your wedding will be one of a kind. Here are some great ideas you can create yourself at home or with the help of your stationer.

SUSANNA MARIE LEWIS
AND
HENRY JAMES WEBBER
CORDIALLY INVITE YOU
TO THE CELEBRATION OF THEIR MARRIAGE
SATURDAY THE FIFTEENTH OF NOVEMBER
TWO THOUSAND AND EIGHT
AT SIX O'CLOCK IN THE EVENING

ST. IGNATIUS CHURCH
100 FULTON STREET
SAN FRANCISCO, CALIFORNIA

RECEPTION IMMEDIATELY FOLLOWING
AT THE FAIRMONT BALLROOM
25 MAIDEN LANE
SAN FRANCISCO, CALIFORNIA

FOLDED INVITATION WITH RIBBON WRAPPER

To showcase your personal style, make invitations that go beyond ordinary expectations. Rather than sending a flat card, try making this three-dimensional paper-fold card with ribbon wrapper. It gives your guests all the information they need—but does it with extra flair. The color contrast is fresh and contemporary, and the sweet polka-dot ribbon adds a whimsical finish. Your guests will truly be impressed when they open this original and clever design.

Here are the materials you will need to make one folded invitation with ribbon wrapper:

- one 4 ½" × 6 ¼" (11.5 × 16 cm) card with rounded corners, natural
- one 5" × 7" (12.5 × 18 cm) pochette folder, cocoa brown
- one 5" × 7" (12.5 × 18 cm) card, light blue
- length of 1 ½" (4 cm) silk ribbon, light blue
- length of ⅝" (1.5 cm) silk ribbon, brown with blue dots
- spray adhesive
- tape

STEP 1.   Print your invitation on the natural card with your color printer or work with your stationer. If you are printing the invitations at home, be sure your card stock is compatible with your home printer.

STEP 2.   With spray adhesive, adhere the light blue card to the inside of the pochette folder. Making sure the cards are centered, adhere the small, natural card with printed information to the light blue card.

STEP 3.   Folding one side at a time, fold over all four flaps of the pochette folder.

STEP 4.   Wrap the wider, blue silk ribbon around the length of the folder. Wrap it tightly enough so it lies flat. Use enough length to create a slight overlap at the ends.

STEP 5.   Secure the overlapped ends with a small piece of tape on the back of the folder. (The tape won't show once you have wrapped the second piece of ribbon.)

STEP 6.   Tie the smaller, polka-dot silk ribbon around the blue ribbon. Secure the ends with a loose knot on the front center of the card.

PLEASE JOIN US
FOR
A BRIDAL
LUNCHEON
IN HONOR OF

ELIZABETH
SEVENER

SATURDAY,
APRIL 4TH
2009
12:00 PM

AT THE HOME
OF
JENNIFER
BUCKLEY

28 CHESTER
PLACE
WILMINGTON,
DELAWARE
(203) 555 0934

PLEASE R.S.V.P
BY
MARCH 28, 2008

MATCHBOOK INVITE

This matchbook invitation is a great example of a new twist on an everyday shape. With a few tiny details and a pop of color, these invitations are the perfect way to send out one-of-a-kind invites with a sophisticated flourish. They are simple and inexpensive to put together, too. You can print up all the information on your color printer at home. Combine prints and solid colors or choose a muted color scheme to create any type of style. Then, just fold them up and pop them in the mail.

Here are the materials you will need to make one matchbook invite:

- one 3 1/4" × 8 3/4" (8.5 × 22 cm) card, white

- one 3 7/8" × 10 1/4" (9.5 × 26 cm) card, light blue

- one 3 1/2" × 9" (9 × 23 cm) card, red

- 1/8" (3 mm)-wide ribbon, cut to 16" (40.5 cm) length

- single-hole punch

PLEASE JOIN US
FOR
A BRIDAL
LUNCHEON
IN HONOR OF

ELIZABETH
SEVENER

SATURDAY,
APRIL 4TH
2009
12:00 PM

AT THE HOME
OF
JENNIFER
BUCKLEY

28 CHESTER
PLACE
WILMINGTON,
DELAWARE
(203) 555-0934

PLEASE R.S.V.P.
BY

MARCH 28, 2008

STEP 1.   Print your invitation on the white card with your color printer. Make sure the event information is printed on the front of the card, at least $1^1/_2$" (4 cm) from the top edge. You can print two cards at once by formatting the document to have two columns. Then split the card in half and trim each to size.

STEP 2.   Make a 1" (2.5 cm) fold at one end of the blue card. Lay the red card on top of the blue card. Then lay the white card on top of the red card, aligning the card ends at the fold.

STEP 3.   Make a pencil mark 1" (2.5 cm) from each side of the fold. Punch two holes through the fold and through the two cards underneath it.

STEP 4.   Feed the ribbon through the holes. Tie the ends at the center to attach all three cards.

STEP 5.   Fold the card up from the bottom. Tuck the end into the top fold to create a "matchbook."

Please Join Us
For a
Beach Party
Celebrating
Amanda
James

BEACH BALL INVITATION

Grab their attention and let them know this wedding is going to be fun! These beach ball invitations are the perfect way to do it. The ceremony doesn't even have to take place on the beach. How about a seaside bridal shower? Or maybe you'd rather have a soccer game at the park. Just mix and match colors for the sport or activity that suits you best. All it takes is a little crafting and imagination. Have a ball!

Here are the materials you will need to make one beach ball invitation:

- round white labels, 1 5/8" (4 cm) in diameter
- round cards, 6" (15 cm) in diameter, in white, red, and blue
- small metal brads
- spray glue
- scissors

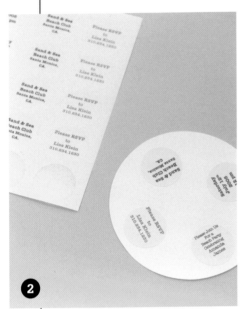

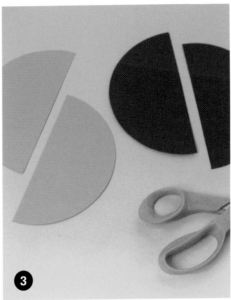

STEP 1. Print your party date, time, and place on the round labels with your
color printer.

STEP 2. Place a printed label in each of the four quadrants of the white card,
as shown in the photo. Be sure the printing is facing outward.

STEP 3. Cut the blue and red circle cards in half.

STEP 4. Cut the blue and red circle card halves in half again.

  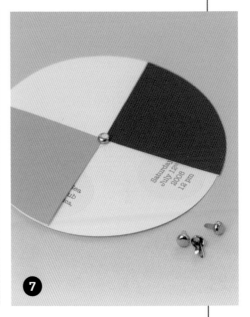

STEP 5.   With the spray glue, glue one red-card quarter and one blue-card quarter onto another white circle card. Be sure the pieces are equally centered on each half and are glued right to the edge of the white card.

STEP 6.   Cut out a section of the white card between the two colored sections. Leave a slight notch of white paper in the center of the card to attach the brad.

STEP 7.   Use the brads to attach the card with colored sections to the white card with party stickers. The top card should spin around to reveal different "windows" that contain all the party details.

More Ideas

RIBBON-TRIMMED INVITATION

Ribbon is a lovely way to embellish just about anything. Whether bright-colored satin or glittery metallic, ribbon always adds the perfect finishing touch.

Wired silver ribbon takes this traditional invitation from simple to spectacular. Just measure the proper length around the card and fold neatly around each corner. Add a dab of glue underneath each fold and strategically place a small bow detail where the ribbon ends meet. Finish with a tiny jewel detail. If you are on a budget, you can easily print up the cards on a home computer and save on printing costs.

STAMPED BORDER INVITATION

Another fast, easy, and great way to embellish invitations is with rubber stamping. There are so many stamp styles and designs to choose from, you won't have any trouble finding one—or more—that suits your style. Look for them at craft shops or scrapbook supplies stores.

Pick a border paper color. Then match your rubber-stamp ink color to the color of your border paper. Scrolls and fleur-de-lis are lovely, traditional designs, but you can choose flowers, dots, or geometric borders, too.

FLORAL-TRIMMED INVITATIONS

Invitations are one of the first ways to establish your wedding's design theme, and florals are an excellent theme choice. A sparkly sequined flower can add drama to a simple design. A light, airy floral can add a dash of romance. You can make these flowery invites either with professionally printed invitations or invitations you make on your own computer. Choose a floral ribbon trim that lies flat against the paper and can be trimmed cleanly at the edges. Be sure not to use trims that are too bulky or you'll need extra postage.

SCROLL-IN-A-TUBE INVITE

There's more than one way to send your invitations. Think outside of the box (or envelope) with these clear, cylindrical tubes. This three-dimensional invite is a fun and fresh spin on everyday stationery.

Print up colorful invitations and roll them up so that the event information shows on the outside of the roll. Then, wrap up the rolls with sparkly streamers or colorful confetti before slipping them inside the tube. Print separate address labels and affix them to the outside of the tube. Be sure you have the right amount of postage before you drop them in the mail. You'll find clear tubes like these at specialty paper stores.

CHAPTER 3

SPECIAL ITEMS FOR SPECIAL EVENTS

Weddings are about more than just one specific event held on one specific day. The celebration is a series of events, and each leads to another until the big day finally arrives. Family and friends come from miles around to celebrate, often staying a few extra days for the festivities. Shower your guests with special treats to welcome them. From bridal showers to brunches and rehearsal dinners, you'll find lots of opportunities to make each gathering special. With a few thoughtful details, you can show everyone why weddings are so much fun—and the perfect way to celebrate love and friendship.

BRIDAL TEA SCRAPBOOK

Scrapbooking is a great way to chronicle your life, tuck away special memories, and create something you and your family will continue to enjoy in years to come. At your bridal tea party, you can invite your guests to actually take part in making your scrapbook. You'll not only have photographs to remember the day, but extra-special memories of the fun you had, too. Everyone has stories or words of advice to share with the bride. With this neat, one-of-a-kind keepsake, you can make sure the message lasts a lifetime.

Here are the materials you will need to make one bridal tea scrapbook:

- plain scrapbook
- assorted scrapbook embellishments and stickers
- colored pens
- assorted photos
- stamps and rubber-stamp ink pad(s)
- decorative paper, cut into 4" × 6" (10 × 15 cm) pieces
- decorative, acid-free adhesive tape

STEP 1.   When sending out your shower invitations, also ask your guests to send you a photo they like of either the bride or groom. Arrange the photos on one or more pages in the scrapbook. Secure the photos with decorative adhesive tape.

STEP 2.   During the shower, supply each guest with a piece of decorative paper and a colored pen. Ask them to write a simple wish, bit of advice, or a haiku dedicated to the bride and groom.

STEP 3.   Collect the pieces of paper. With adhesive tape, arrange the pieces around the photos in the scrapbook to make captions.

STEP 4.   Ask your guests to select stamps, stickers, or other embellishments and take turns decorating the finished page.

Try this!

Make a game out of who can write the best poem. Award the winner a prize—and be sure to include the poem on the scrapbook page.

WELCOME CANDY BAG

Guests gladly come from far and wide to celebrate the marriage of two people they love. These welcoming candy bags are a sweet and simple gesture to let your guests know you're happy they made the trip. They're easy to make, so you can whip them up in no time for any gathering—from the rehearsal dinner to the farewell brunch. Choose papers, ribbons, and embellishments that tie in to your theme or special style. Fill them to the brim with your favorite treats for everyone to enjoy.

Here are the materials you will need to make one candy bag:

- one cellophane candy bag, approximately 10" × 4 3/4" (25.5 × 12 cm)

- one piece of patterned paper, 4 3/4" × 12" (12 × 30.5 cm)

- length of 3/8" (1 cm)-wide ribbon

- one paper tag, 1" × 3" (2.5 × 7.5 cm)

- small wrapped candies, various selections of your choice

STEP 1.   Make a fold 2$\frac{1}{2}$" (6.5 cm) from the bottom of the patterned paper. Slide the paper into the cellophane bag. The fold will create a flat bottom for the bag.

STEP 2.   Fill the bag with the desired amount of a selection of wrapped candies.

STEP 3.   Trim the top of the cellophane bag to the same height as the top of the patterned paper. Fold both over 1" (2.5 cm).

STEP 4.   Secure the bag by tying the ribbon around the width of the bag to enclose the fold.

STEP 5. Write the word "Welcome" on your tag with a colored pen or pencil.

STEP 6. Feed the welcome tag through one end of the ribbon and secure with a small bow.

Try this!

Instead of tying the bag with a ribbon, simply close the bag at the back with a small piece of transparent tape.

More Ideas

BACHELORETTE SCAVENGER HUNT SCROLL

Host a bachelorette scavenger hunt! This type of party can be tailor-made to suit any bride's tastes and interests—whether she's into music, nightlife, sports, or quiet nights at home. Hand out a copy of the list to every guest, with items ranging from a kiss from a stranger to a movie-ticket stub. Set a time limit and award points for each item collected (guests can "collect" some items simply by snapping a digital image). Work in teams to give the race an edge. A prize is a must, even if it's just bragging rights.

AFTER-THE-WEDDING-BRUNCH NEWSPAPER WRAPPER

Before the newlyweds take off for their honeymoon and the out-of-town guests head home, it's fun to get together for an after-the-wedding brunch. Give everyone one last keepsake: a copy of the daily newspaper—but with your wedding as the headline news! Make a color copy of the front page of your local paper and paste a color photo of the bride and groom front and center. Print out and paste a headline in place: "They Finally Did It!" or "Happy Couple Takes the Plunge!" Wrap the new front page around the paper with a ribbon. Your wedding really is front-page news!

OUT-OF-TOWNERS' NAME TAGS

Make sure everyone gets to know one another by providing these easy-to-make name tags. They're a great conversation starter and will put everyone at ease as they get acquainted.

Specify whether the guest is from the bride's or groom's side. Add extra information, too, such as "Best Man" or "Favorite Uncle." If you're having a destination wedding, include each guest's hometown as well.

You'll find ready-to-print name tags at office supplies stores, complete with computer templates. Scan a cute illustration from a book or find clip art on the Internet to personalize.

REHEARSAL DINNER COASTER

These coasters are easy and inexpensive to make. Just make or buy a stack of simple paper circles (which you'll find at any art supplies store or stationery shop). Choose a rubber stamp with the image of a bride and groom and a date stamp, too. Or select a simple floral or decorative stamp in your color scheme. These small extras will impress your guests with little effort and big style.

REHEARSAL DINNER PHOTO BOARD

Encourage friends and family to share stories, advice, and best wishes by making a photo board that you can post nearby the rehearsal dinner table.

To get things started, attach baby pictures of the bride and groom. Leave enough space around the photos for everyone to write a line or two. Hand out colored markers and metallic pens and watch the board fill up.

CHAPTER 4

PLACE CARDS

Flowers and candles are wonderful, but don't underestimate the power of paper details. The smallest items on the tables at your wedding events can say so much about you and your personal style. Make the table a special environment your guests will enjoy. Create place settings that sparkle with glitter and jewels. Tie your place cards to your wedding theme and design. Number the tables with clever keepsake frames. Discover creative ways to guide your guests to their seats. These small details say a lot about you—and will make your guests feel pampered and special, too.

DÉCOUPAGE TABLE-NUMBER FRAME

Table numbers should help your guests find their assigned seating, but they can also add a little flair to your table décor. With a quick and clever technique, you can assemble these adorable keepsake découpage frames. Choose a style that complements your table's colors and theme. Invite a few girlfriends over for a craft night to make as many frames as you need—a great way to have a laugh with your friends while getting ready for the big day. These frames are so charming, guests will fight over who gets to take one home!

Here are the materials you will need to make one découpage table-number frame:

- one small wooden frame, unfinished, approximately 6" × 8" (15 × 20.5 cm), with an opening that is approximately 3" × 4½" (7.5 × 11.5 cm)

- one card or piece of colored paper, for table number, just slightly larger than the frame opening

- one small sheet of patterned floral paper (a design with large flowers that are easy to cut out works best)

- scissors

- whitewash paint

- découpage glue

- small paintbrush

STEP 1.   Handwrite the table number on the center of the card or colored paper. You can also print the number with your computer and home printer.

STEP 2.   Paint the entire frame with whitewash paint. Allow the paint to dry.

STEP 3.   Cut out large flower shapes from the patterned paper. Set the flowers aside.

STEP 4.   Arrange the paper flowers around the frame.

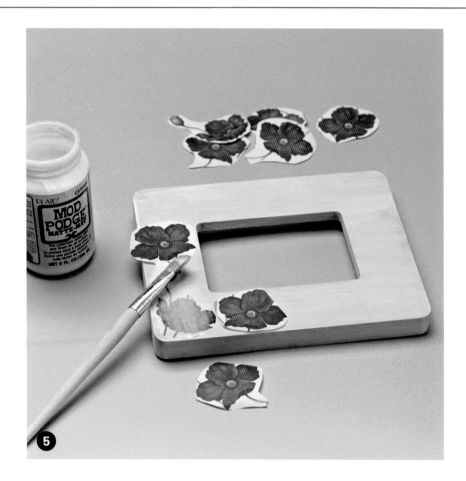

STEP 5.   Working with the découpage glue and paintbrush, adhere each flower, one at a time, onto the frame. Apply glue liberally until each flower is saturated with glue and attached securely to the frame. Découpage glue dries clear, so you can use as much as you need—it won't show.

STEP 6.   Allow the frame to dry completely. Then insert the table number into the frame opening.

CORRUGATED NAPKIN RING PLACE CARD

Corrugated papers lend an understated style to your table settings—the perfect casual look for the modern bride who wants to express her own one-of-a-kind point of view. The natural white and soft brown shades of the papers tie in beautifully with an assortment of dried flowers and stems to create, dramatic, earthy style. Simple flowers like calla lilies work nicely, too. Add a dash of color by swapping the natural raffia tie for a bright cord or ribbon.

Corrugated paper and raffia come in large rolls, so you will probably have enough to decorate many tables. The tags come in packages of 8 to 50, so be sure to buy the correct amount for your needs.

Here are the materials you will need to make one corrugated napkin ring place card and to cover one vase and one votive:

• one roll of brown corrugated paper
• one roll of white corrugated paper
• one napkin
• one spool of natural-colored raffia
• one oval-shaped tag
• one tall, cylindrical glass vase
• one small glass votive
• scissors
• double-stick tape
• tape measure

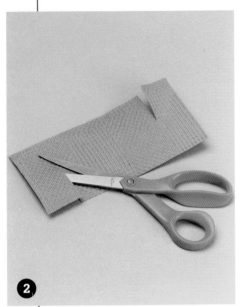

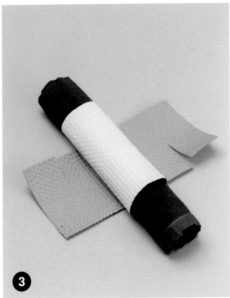

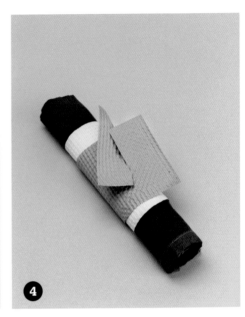

STEP 1.   Cut one 3 1/2" × 8" (9 × 20.5 cm) piece of brown corrugated paper.

Cut one 5" × 5" (12.5 × 12.5 cm) piece of white corrugated paper.

STEP 2.   Cut a 1 3/4" (4.5 cm)-long slit in the brown paper, 1 1/2" (4 cm) in from each end.

STEP 3.   Wrap the white corrugated paper around the middle of the napkin. Then wrap the brown corrugated paper around the center of the white paper.

STEP 4.   Slide the two slits together to join the ends of the brown paper.

STEP 5.   Wrap the raffia two or three times around the napkin, leaving a long tail. Cut the strand from the spool, leaving another long tail.

STEP 6.   Feed one end of the raffia strand through a name tag. Tie a knot to secure the tag.

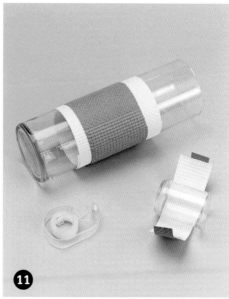

STEP 7.   Fray both ends of the raffia by splitting the fibers of the tails.

STEP 8.   Measure the diameter of your vase and votive with a tape measure. Cut out a piece of white paper, as wide as the diameter of the vase, allowing a little extra for overlap at the ends. Cut another piece of white paper, as wide as the diameter of the votive, allowing a little extra for overlap at the ends.

STEP 9.   Secure the white paper to the vase with double-sided tape. Secure the white paper to the votive the same way.

STEP 10.   Cut out pieces of brown paper as you did for the white paper in step 8, making the pieces slightly narrower than the white paper.

STEP 11.   Repeat step 9 with the brown paper.

STEP 12.   Wrap the raffia two or three times around the vase, leaving a long tail. Cut the strand from the spool, leaving another long tail. Tie a knot and then fray the ends as you did in step 7.

More Ideas

MINI VASE PLACE CARD

Here's a charming place card that is also an integral part of the table décor. Choose a colorful array of small posies and arrange them in a pretty vase. Write your guest's name and table number on a card and tie it to the vase. Not only do you have a cheery table accent, as an added bonus, you have a great party favor for each guest, too.

VELLUM PLACE CARD

Vellum paper is a translucent paper that will add soft, old-world elegance to the pattern and color scheme of your table settings. If you're working with a bright accent color, choose a patterned card paper that coordinates with that color. Add a solid white vellum paper as an overlay. Print the names of your guests right on the vellum—perhaps with gold or silver ink. Cut the vellum to the same size as the place card, punch a hole in each, and secure the vellum to the front of the card with a lovely textured or patterned ribbon.

SEASHELL PLACE CARD

Planning a summer wedding? The decorating possibilities are endless. Why not start with these fun and casual seashell cards? They are super easy to make and add the perfect seaside touch to your tables—whether you're actually seaside or not! Either handwrite your guests' names on each card or print them onto clear labels with your computer printer. Then, simply glue a few small seashells to the corner of each card. Tie a bow with a bit of colored raffia and glue it to the top of the card to nicely complement your color scheme.

CLOTHESPIN SEATING CHART

Here's a handy way to figure out who should sit where. With this clothespin table number board, you can mix and match guests and tables with ease. Make individual tags with each table number and guest's name. (Use small tags for the table number and longer ones for the names.) Handwrite them or print them from your computer. Or, for super style, hire a calligrapher to hand-letter them in a decorative script.

Cover a small bulletin board with fabric and attach colored ribbons that span from side to side. (Be sure to attach the ribbons securely so they withstand all the pulling and moving of the tags as you sort things out.) Display the board on a table where your guests can find it easily. What a charming way to guide them to their seats!

MINI FRAME PLACE CARD

Place cards are a necessity at any wedding reception to organize the seating. These mini frame place cards are so sweet, your guests will also cherish them as mementoes to take home and use another day. You'll find many styles of miniature frames at craft and party stores. Choose one that matches your theme, and then add a little bit of personality. Pressed flowers come in a variety of colors and styles and are simple to glue onto most surfaces. Silver frames, white flowers, or small sparkles create a shinier, more formal look.

JEWELED PLACE CARD

Dazzle your guests with the bedazzling details on these sparkly, jeweled place cards. Set on black paper, small jewels— of any color—and fine, fluffy feathers really pop out and make an impression. Experiment with sequins and a bit of silk or satin, too. Decorate the tables with silver balls, strings of silver garland, elegant flowers, and candles to complete the look. If you want a splash of color, add roses in a deep red or vibrant pink. These dramatic place cards are simple to make—and a fabulous way to dress up the tables at an evening reception.

Once upon a time there was a boy named
Benjamin and he was a fine boy. He went
to college, got a job and worked very hard.
One day he went out to a magical place
called Long Island, where he met what he
considered to be a princess named Hailey.
They instantly fell in love and decided to
get married.
Today, we gather together to celebrate that
marriage in front of Benjamin and

Hailey's dearest
Gayle and Larry
give their daughter
Harris joins these two
Harriet and Mitch
reading to honor the marr...
we, Jennifer Kellen and
will stand witness as this
The rest is just the beginning

"Once Upon a
time…"

The love story of Hailey and
Benjamin

...tober 18, 2008

CHAPTER 5

PROGRAMS AND DISPLAYS

Wedding plans are all about communication. Getting guests to and fro, directing them from one place to the next, and keeping them informed about activities and events can be a full-time job. Keep on top of it all by creating some clear and clever signage, programs, and displays. Add a little extra touch, and what starts out as a simple list of names can become a meaningful keepsake for you and your guests. Choose whimsical shapes and bold and beautiful colors and designs to lead the way from cocktails to dinner. Let photographs speak a thousand words and transform simple sheets of paper into cherished memories.

September 12, 2008

The Marriage of
Susanna Marie Williams
To
Jonathan Thomas Carter

Officiated by

Rev. Jeffrey Simon

Bridal Attendants

Harriet Foster
Lisa Timmons
Barbara Roth

Groomsmen

Timothy Bracy
Peter Hoffman
John North

Readers

Gayle Hoffman
Kendall Randall
Robert Moss

PROGRAM FAN

These sweet program fans are useful, too. They let your guests know who's in the wedding party and what will happen during the ceremony. They also provide a handy source of cool relief if your event happens to fall on a hot summer day! These program fans are simple to assemble and custom-style with any combinations of colors, paper, and ribbon you choose. If you don't have a planned program, why not print up a love poem on the fan instead? There's no doubt this is a wonderful keepsake your guests will appreciate.

Here are the materials you will need to make one program fan:

- one 8 $\frac{1}{2}$" × 11" (21.5 × 28 cm) sheet of colored paper
- one 12" × 12" (30.5 × 30.5 cm) sheet of card stock or heavy craft paper
- one 8" (20.5 cm) length of ribbon
- spray mount adhesive
- pinking shears
- single-hole punch

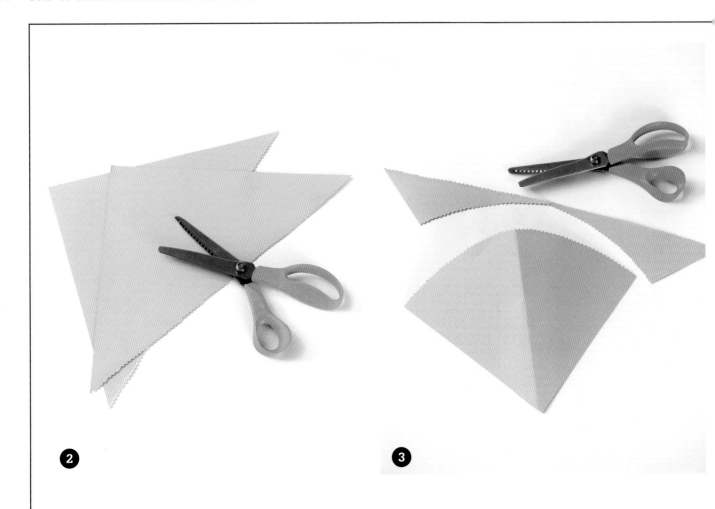

STEP 1.   Working with your home computer and printer, print your program or poem in the center of the sheet of colored paper.

STEP 2.   Fold the large sheet of card stock in half diagonally. Cut along the fold with the pinking shears.

STEP 3.   Fold one triangular piece in half again. With the pinking shears, trim the top of the fan to form a soft curve. If necessary, trim the fan at the top of the center fold to smooth the curved edge.

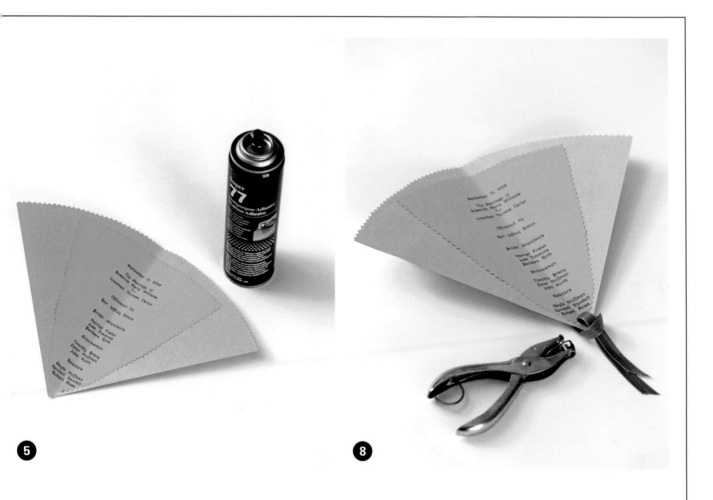

STEP 4. Cut the sheet with the poem or program into a triangle that will fit inside the fan. Be sure to carefully center the printed sheet so as not to trim off any of the information.

STEP 5. With the spray adhesive, adhere the smaller triangle to the center of the larger one.

STEP 6. With the single-hole punch, punch a hole in the bottom point of the fan.

STEP 7. Fold the ribbon in half lengthwise. Feed the two ends through the hole in the fan.

STEP 8. Pull the ends through the loop at the other end of the folded ribbon. Pull gently to secure the ribbon to the end of the fan.

PRESSED-FLOWER VOW HOLDER

The friends and family members you've chosen to be a part of your wedding are an important part of your life. Present them with a keepsake to commemorate the day they helped make special. This sweet holder is a lovely way for them to carry the poem or passage they'll read during the ceremony. Make two more for you and your spouse to carry your wedding vows. With delicate paper or vellum, a few pressed flowers, and silk ribbon, you can transform a few fleeting words into a lasting treasure.

Here are the materials you will need to make one pressed-flower vow holder:

- one 10" × 12" (25.5 × 30.5 cm) sheet of delicate natural-fiber paper or vellum
- one 8 1/2" × 11" (21.5 × 28 cm) sheet of card stock, off white
- one 8 1/2" × 11" (21.5 × 28 cm) sheet of paper, white or color of your choice
- pressed flowers
- length of 5/8" (1.5 cm)-wide silk ribbon
- spray adhesive

STEP 1.   Spray the card stock lightly with adhesive. Place the natural-fiber paper or vellum on top of it. Smooth out any bubbles or folds.

STEP 2.   Trim the edges of the paper and card so they are even. Fold the two sheets together in half lengthwise.

STEP 3.   Handwrite or print out the poem, passage, or vows on a sheet of paper. Be sure to position the writing so that the ribbon won't obscure the words when it's tied in place. Fold the paper in half and place it inside the folder.

STEP 4.   Pull the ribbon through the center fold and tie it in front of the folder, securing the sheet of writing inside.

STEP 5.   Glue small pressed flowers onto the front of the holder. Allow the glue to dry thoroughly.

More Ideas

PHOTO PROGRAM

Guests are always curious about who's who in the wedding party. The bride and groom are the stars of the show, but what about all of those fabulous supporting players? Shine the spotlight on all those people who played a role in your special event. Print a photograph of each one of them on the wedding program. Include each name and a little description of who the person is and the contributions that he or she made to the big day. Be sure to add some sweet or funny stories or bits of trivia, too. This thoughtful touch will make your day—and theirs—picture perfect!

COCKTAIL HOUR SIGNAGE

People sometimes need a little help to get where they're going—especially when there are lots of interesting people and exciting activities to distract them. This Cocktail Hour sign will point your thirsty guests in the right direction. It's very easy to assemble and sturdy enough to hang almost anywhere with a little heavy, double-sided tape or fishing line. All you'll need is some poster board, a box of sparkly letters, and a little bit of imagination to add one-of-a-kind flair to your day. Let the celebrations begin!

GIFT TABLE DISPLAY

Here's a clever and whimsical way to direct your guests to the gift table, no questions asked. Wrap up the sign to blend in with the gifts themselves. Tailor the idea for bridal showers or bachelorette parties by simply switching the pattern and style of the wrapping paper, ribbon, and bow. No one will mistake this adorable sign for a present, but it will certainly do the trick.

STORYBOOK PROGRAM

"Once upon a time, a boy and a girl fell in love. . . ." The story of how you and your spouse-to-be got to this special day is a sweet subject for a wedding program. Start out with the basics, such as how the two of you met. After you've set the stage, add some new characters—for example, the family and friends in the wedding party. Finally, add a little bit about what your guests will hear and see during the ceremony. Maybe end with a special thought, poem, or wish. Remember, today's love story is just the beginning of a long life of happily-ever-after.

DECORATIVE MAP AND DIRECTIONS

You don't want your guests to get lost on their way to the big event. Draw some simple, clear maps to help them stay on course. They'll appreciate the help. Many mapping websites will provide a street map of your town or neighborhood. Print out several copies and glue them to standard-size postcards to enclose with your wedding invitations. Highlight with a marker all of the different spots of interest—including the location of the reception, their hotel, and a few can't-miss attractions for out-of-towners.

CHAPTER 6

PERSONAL TOUCHES

Those small personal touches—so much fun to design and so easy to add—will make your wedding a truly one-of-a-kind event. With just a little imagination, you'll find plenty of ways to express yourself, in even the simplest details. Everything from the first invitation to the last thank-you card should showcase your style. Create a special keepsake by making a fun guestbook or a beautiful petal toss. Thank your guests with thoughtful notes that have a little extra flourish. The personal touches you choose will make your day uniquely special. The memories will last long after the party is over.

PETAL-TOSS CONE

At one time, people tossed rice at the bride and groom, symbolizing their wishes for the couple's good luck and prosperity in the marriage. Your guests can take part in this longtime wedding tradition by gently showering the happy couple with rose petals from these sweet and simple cones. You could also fill the cones with fresh lavender flowers or birdseed if you'd prefer. All are eco-friendly. No matter which you choose, you'll leave behind traces of a beautiful and lasting memory.

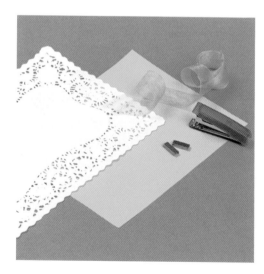

Here are the materials you will need to make one petal-toss cone:

- white paper doily, 10" × 14 $^1\!/_2$" (25.5 × 37 cm)
- vellum paper, 8 $^1\!/_2$" × 11" (21.5 × 28 cm)
- small stapler
- length of ribbon, in width and color of your choice
- fresh flower petals, dried flowers, or birdseed

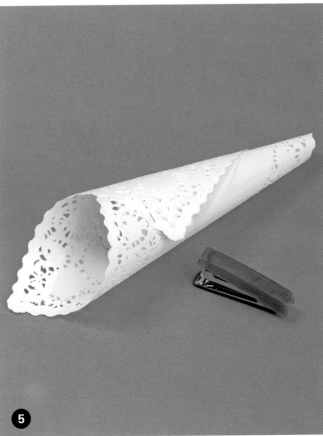

STEP 1.   Lay the vellum paper on top of the doily.

STEP 2.   Starting at one corner, roll the two paper sheets at the same time to
begin to form a cone.

STEP 3.   Staple the bottom of the partial cone to hold it securely in place.

STEP 4.   Continue rolling the paper until you have rolled it all and formed a
large cone.

STEP 5.   Staple the overlapping layers of the doily at the top of the cone—
close to the corner—to hold the cone securely.

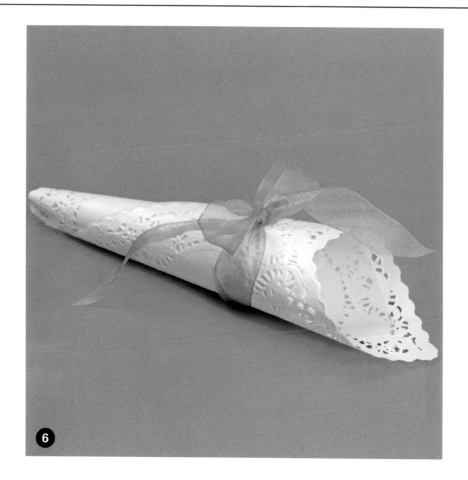

STEP 6.   Tie your ribbon loosely around the cone to form a bow. Position the bow so it hides the top staple.

STEP 7.   Fill the cones with fresh flower petals, dried flowers, or birdseed— your choice!

Try this!

Store fresh flower petals in the refrigerator to keep them fresh and fill the cones on the day of the wedding.

BUTTON-FLOWER THANK-YOU NOTE

When friends and family members come from miles around to celebrate your special day, usually bearing generous gifts, it's important—and polite—to thank them properly. Go the extra mile and take the time to create a one-of-a-kind card. Your effort will let them know how much you truly care and appreciate their love and support. Get creative with everyday items, such as colorful or novelty buttons, and your cards will be inexpensive to make and send. (Just be sure to add the right amount of postage.)

Here are the materials you will need to make one button-flower thank-you note:

- one 3 1/2" × 5" (9 × 12.5 cm) fold-over card with envelope
- rubber stamp embossed with the message "Thanks" or "Thank you"
- brown ink pad
- six small silk leaves, with stems approximately 1" (2.5 cm) long
- craft glue
- three buttons in a mix of colors

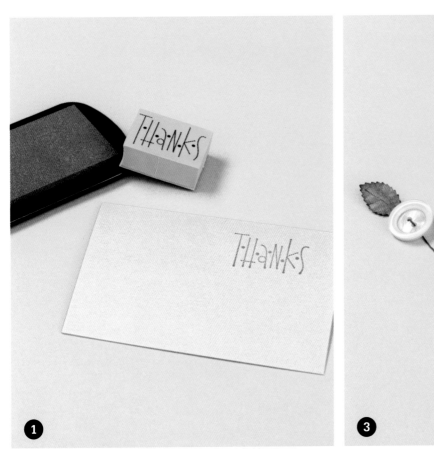

STEP 1. Working with the rubber stamp and the brown ink pad, firmly stamp the message in the upper right-hand corner of the fold-over card.

STEP 2. Fold one leaf slightly on its stem. Glue this leaf on the card. Make sure the leaf does not hang off the side of the card. The stem should reach the bottom edge.

STEP 3. Feed the stem of one of the leaves up and through one of the buttons.

STEP 4.   Fold the remaining end of the stem behind the button so only the leaf
is sticking out.

STEP 5.   Glue the button with the attached leaf onto the leaf that is already glued
to the card. There should be a leaf on both sides of the button, to create
the button flower.

STEP 6.   Repeat steps 2 through 5, first on the right side of the card and then
at the center. When you've finished, you'll have three cheery flowers
"growing" on the front of your thank-you note. Add your message inside.

More Ideas

STAMPED NAPKIN

There's no easier or quicker craft than rubber stamping. You can buy all sorts of letters in a variety of sizes and styles at most craft stores. You can also find stamps with border prints and other decorative details. For fun, you might want to stamp a wedding cake, bells, or a bride and groom onto napkins, too.

Choose solid paper napkins that match the color scheme and style of your wedding events. Choose an ink pad in a contrasting color so the lettering and designs pop off the paper. Include some stenciling to add extra dimension and interest. They may be small, but these decorative details make a big impression.

PHOTO THANK-YOU CARD

Share your digital memories with your guests—including those who couldn't attend—by sending these photo thank-yous. Pick your favorite shot of the bride and groom. Gather a few sheets of patterned scrapbook paper (or wrapping paper) and some plain, folded cards. Cut a square of paper smaller than the card but larger than your photo. Glue the square to the card front and mount the photo at the center of the square to create a patterned "frame." You can also download and print photo stickers from photo-sharing websites.

MONOGRAMMED CARD

Say thank you with style. These simple monogrammed cards look expensive and sophisticated, but they are quick, easy, and affordable. Stamp your new monogram with an ink color that complements the paper color. Monograms are usually three letters: the initial letter of your first name, the initial letter of your spouse's first name, and in the center, the initial letter of your last name (if it's shared). If you are keeping your maiden name, just add a fourth letter. Decorate the card with scraps of wrapping paper—how about the paper from your wedding gifts?—to add extra flair.

FISHBOWL OF BEST WISHES

Here's a clever take on the traditional guestbook—and a cute way to gather bits of advice and best wishes. Cut up decorative papers into small cards that are large enough for your guests to write you a few lines. Choose a variety of paper colors and styles that match your theme or décor.

Drop the cards into a large fishbowl or a deep glass bowl. Set the bowl on a small table in the reception area, with a cup of colored pens or pencils nearby, to encourage guests to dip in. Once you're home, read a few every day. The glow of your wedding will linger for weeks. Save the cards in a keepsake scrapbook or photo album so you can reread them again and again.

SCRAPBOOK GUESTBOOK

Instead of just collecting names, make the most of this guestbook by turning it into a keepsake filled with sketches, sayings, and signatures.

Start with a plain, bound scrapbook in the color and style you like best. Display it along with a tray full of stickers, stamps, colored pens, and other scrapbooking tools. Friends and family will stand in line to express their best wishes and add their own special touches to your memory book.

CHAPTER 7

PAPER DÉCOR

Whenever you decorate a room, you are creating an environment that is infused with your personality. It shows in the colors you choose, the ideas you prefer, and the way you put all the elements together. Whether you are designing a bridal shower, rehearsal dinner, or the wedding ceremony itself, there are countless ways you can make each of your events a one-of-a-kind occasion.

The first step is to be sure your style and enthusiasm are on display in every detail you choose, whether you're creating a unique centerpiece, a display of paper lanterns, or a festive banner. Match your paper-craft extras to the colors, themes, and ideas you've chosen for your special day. Everywhere they look, your guests will see your style shining through.

COCKTAIL STIRRERS

Weddings stir up sweet emotions—but why not stir up some fun, too? These personalized cocktail stirrers will spice up every beverage. Design a signature cocktail to serve at the reception. Think of something fresh and easy that goes with your décor or theme. If pink is your color, add a splash of grenadine. Are you planning a summer event? Rum-based mojitos are easy to serve and always a big hit. Add your one-of-a-kind stirrers, and you'll give your guests something to admire as they're sipping their fabulous beverages.

Here are the materials you will need to make approximately 100 cocktail stirrers:

- computer-printable mailing labels, about 1" × 2 ⅝" (2.5 × 6.5 cm)
- one package of wooden skewers (50 count)
- two sheets of small-patterned scrapbooking paper, 8 ½" × 11" (21.5 × 28 cm)
- scissors or snips
- double-stick tape
- pinking shears

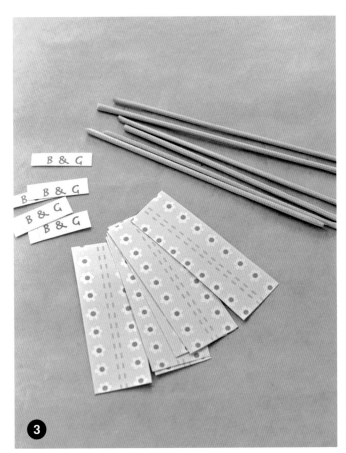

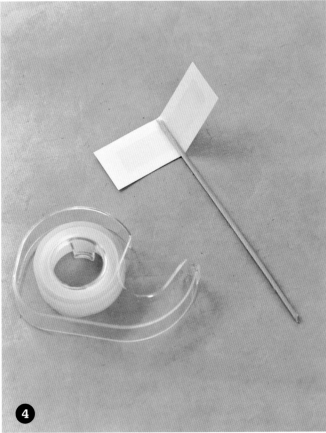

STEP 1.   Print as many monograms as will fit on each label, in the color of your choice. (We used 1" × 2 5/8" [2.5 × 6.5 cm] off-white labels and fit six monograms in 20-point font on each label.) Cut out all the monograms to make individual stickers.

STEP 2.   Cut the skewers in half with sturdy kitchen scissors or garden snips. Or trim the length of the skewer to fit a shorter glass, if preferred.

STEP 3.   Cut one hundred 1" × 2.5" (2.5 × 6.5 cm) strips from the sheets of patterned paper with the scissors or snips.

STEP 4.   Fold a strip of patterned paper in half. Adhere a strip of double-sided tape to the underside of the patterned paper. Place a skewer into the fold of the paper. Press together the two taped halves to make a small flag.

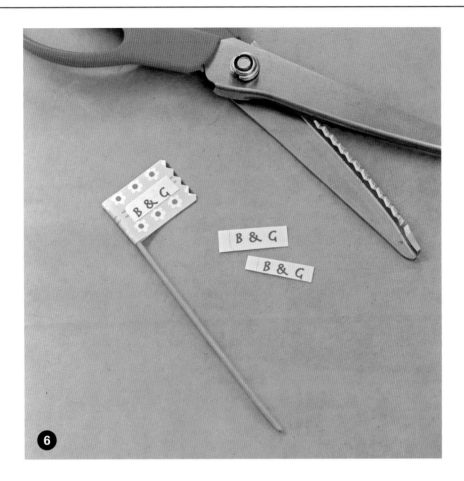

STEP 5.   Peel the back off one of the monogram stickers. Adhere it to the center of the flag. Add another monogram to the other side.

STEP 6.   With pinking shears, trim the flag to make a neat and decorative edge.

Try this!

Make a sample stirrer to make sure you have a good length for your glass. If the stirrer is too long, it's easy to trim it later to make it shorter—but if it's too short, you'll have to start again.

More Ideas

LANTERN VASE

Here's a super-bold and colorful tablescape. Buy these inexpensive paper lanterns at specialty and party supply stores. Just remove the tassels from the bottoms of the lanterns so that the lanterns will sit flat on the tabletop. Cut small slits in the top opening of each lantern so you can place a vase inside. Insert the vase and then secure the lantern to the top of the vase with a small bit of double-sided tape or floral wire. Fill the vases with your favorite bright flowers, and your tabletop will pop!

MATCHBOXES AND VOTIVES

Dress up small table items to quickly and easily add festive flair. These clever decorations also double as sweet keepsakes for guests to take away at the end of the day.

Choose papers that complement your color scheme but are different enough to stand out. Wrapping paper works well and offers a wide range of colors, patterns, and textures. Display your decorative votives and matching matchboxes on side tables near the cocktail table, in a small sitting area, or in an outdoor space to liven up these out-of-the way spots. If you prefer, you can replace the matchboxes with small boxes of mints or other treats.

FESTIVE BANNER

Wrap some whimsy around your wedding events with a fun and festive banner. These paper accents are easy to construct and add a little something extra to any space.

Simply cut out several paper triangles and glue them to a long string or ribbon. Give these old-fashioned festoons a contemporary twist by choosing funky papers and decorative designs. String the banners—of any length—in doorways, archways, or across a wall.

TISSUE PAPER FLOWERS

Who needs real flowers when you can have fun faux flowers like these? No refrigeration needed!

Stack six pieces of tissue paper, cut to equal size. Cut the stack in half. Each half will make one flower. Fold each half accordion style in 1" (2.5 cm) folds. Fasten the center with a pipe cleaner in a matching color. Cut the paper ends in curves to resemble large petals.

Lay the accordion folds flat and pull layers toward the center, two layers at a time. Fluff the petals as needed. Choose multicolored tissues for an eye-popping effect or muted colors for a softer scheme.

CUTOUT TABLE LANTERN

Here's a soft, organic detail to add a sweet and subtle touch to your wedding-day theme. Choose muted natural papers and look for paper punches with natural shapes—leaves, flowers, or stars, to name a few of the many choices. Punch the shapes from the paper. Then wrap the paper around a vase, trimming the paper to size at the top and bottom. Secure the paper with double-sided tape. Fill the vase with flowers or place a candle in it to create a lantern. The candlelight will flicker through the pretty punched shapes, streaming small rays of light onto your special day.

HANGING STARS

Make a little magic! Transform colorful paper bags into delightful hanging stars. So simple in style and so easy to make, these stars are perfect accents for any special occasion. They also make easy décor for destination weddings because they fold flat until you're ready to hang them. Paper bags are available in craft stores in a wide variety of colors and sizes. If your event has a black-and-white color scheme, mix it up by using three bags of each color to create a dramatic pinwheel effect. To complete the look, hang the stars with a bold, black-and-white-striped ribbon. You can make multicolor stars the same way, too.

PART II
FAUX FLORALS & CANDLES

Flowers of all sorts, exchanged by couples as tokens of love, have a deep resonance in our romantic lives. So, naturally, their beauty, form, color, and meaning play a central part in wedding ceremonies and celebrations. From the bridal bouquet to the reception room décor, flowers help make the most of the special day.

Today's brides can choose from a wide array of faux flower varieties and designs. Some may prefer a traditional bouquet of white roses. Others might choose bright magenta dahlias wrapped in ivy or a mix of springtime pastels wrapped in decorative trim.

Candles, in a variety of shapes, sizes, and colors, are another wedding essential. You can showcase candles in many creative ways—from the lighting of the marriage candle to the twilight illumination of a garden path to the design of an elegant centerpiece.

Here are some ideas for matching your wedding flowers and candles with your unique style and personality. Consider the time of day, the time of year, the location, and your theme, too. Your thoughtful choices will transform your wedding into a truly one-of-a kind event.

CHAPTER 8

WARM WELCOMES

Friends and relatives travel from near and far to be a part of your special day. Why not plan a fun event to extend a warm welcome? Have a barbecue, a cocktail party on the beach, a girls' luncheon, or a thank-you brunch. Welcome gatherings are all about having fun, so keep them light and breezy. Everyone will appreciate the casual feeling and the chance to relax before the big event. Choose a theme or add a game, activity, or another sort of fun-filled twist, but remember: Keep it simple and low-key. The big party is still to come!

BRIDAL TEACUP ARRANGEMENT

Here's a sweet and special, one-of-a-kind favor that your shower or wedding guests will treasure for years to come. This flower-filled teacup is a unique memento to thank friends and relatives for sharing your day. If you want a uniform look and style, buy as many of the same cups as you have guests. Or, for a little variety, hunt through thrift shops and home stores and gather together an assortment of decorative patterns and styles. Either way, these clever giveaways are charming!

Here are the materials you will need to make one bridal teacup:

- one teacup and matching saucer
- one block of floral foam
- three stems of white carnations
- two stems of white spray roses
- three stems of white apple blossoms
- floral snips

STEP 1.   Cut the floral foam to fit inside the teacup, leaving about $\frac{1}{2}$" (1.3 cm) of foam extending above the rim. Be sure the surface is level. Push down firmly to ensure a snug fit.

STEP 2.   Snip the carnation stems to a 2" (5 cm) length.

STEP 3.   Insert the stems around the side of the teacup and toward the center so that the blossoms cover some of the side. Push down at an angle to ensure the stems are firmly in the foam. Space the carnations evenly around the circumference of the teacup to fill in.

STEP 4.   Snip the spray roses to a 5" (12.5 cm) length. Place the roses into the foam in a circular arrangement around the teacup. Make sure the roses are slightly higher than the carnation petals, creating a mound. Fill in all the way around. For more texture, add some buds.

STEP 5.   To make the final layer, cut the apple blossoms to a 6" (15 cm) length. Fill the center with apple blossoms. Be sure the heads are just above the roses to complete the dome shape. If the stems aren't rigid enough, wrap them with a length of floral wire before inserting them in the foam.

Try this!

To make a permanent arrangement, affix the saucer to the cup with ceramic adhesive before you begin. Let the adhesive dry and then make the floral arrangement.

BLOOMING TIER

This flirty arrangement is a tower of texture and color. No matter what the season, it sings of spring. This elegant and dramatic arrangement is perfect for a bridal shower, a welcome reception, or a brunch. The clustered layers of blossoms, arranged in concentric circles, create the old-fashioned look and style of a Victorian nosegay. Select any type of small-blossomed flower in the shades you like best. Apple blossoms, sweet peas, and grape hyacinths are all lovely choices.

Here are the materials you will need to make one blooming tier:

- two 6" (15 cm) terra-cotta pots
- one block of floral foam
- three terra-cotta saucers, one in each size: 4" (10 cm), 6" (15 cm), and 8" (20.5 cm)
- three bunches of mini irises
- three bunches of mini daffodils
- two bunches of tulips
- six to eight leaves from tulip bunches
- hot-glue gun and glue sticks
- floral snips
- floral wire

STEP 1.   Turn one pot upside down and center it on the largest saucer. Hot-glue the pot in place. Next, hot-glue the medium-size saucer on top of the base of the glued pot. Hot-glue the smallest saucer on top of that, upside down. Finally, glue the second pot onto the upside-down saucer. Let the terra-cotta tiers dry thoroughly.

STEP 2.   Cut the floral foam into small rectangular blocks. Glue the blocks onto the lip of the bottom pot.

STEP 3.   Continue gluing foam onto the second tier. Cut foam to shape to fill the top pot. Trim all the corners that stick out past the edges.

STEP 4.   Cut iris stems to 2" (5 cm) in length and hot-glue them into the foam. Arrange the flowers around the base, keeping the heads even. If a stem sticks out too far, simply cut the stem and try again.

STEP 5. Just as you did for the iris, cut the daffodil stems to 2" (5 cm) in length and glue them around the second tier. Be sure the tier is filled in with blossoms to create a full and rounded look.

STEP 6. Arrange the tulips in the top pot, trimming the stems as needed to get the height and shape you like. Start positioning the flowers at the center of the pot, making those stems the longest. Work out to the sides, trimming the stems to length so the flowers form a slight dome shape.

STEP 7. After you've added all the tulips, fold each leaf in half, base to tip, to create a loop. Wrap the ends of the leaf together with floral wire. Push the wire securely into the foam in the top pot. Arrange folded leaves around the entire outside of the pot to add a final layer of color, texture, and interest to the tier.

More Ideas

BEACHSIDE HURRICANES

A sunset wedding is magical—especially when the sun is setting over the ocean. Here's a natural decorative detail that can create an over-the-top romantic effect. Pour a small amount of sand into tall glass candleholders of any shape. Position a white or neutral-colored pillar candle securely in the sand. Next, add a random selection of pretty shells, colorful bits of sea glass, and other ocean treasures, such as starfish or small pieces of driftwood (you can find all of these in craft and floral supply stores). Scatter more shells and sea glass around the candleholder to complete the tablescape.

ALL-AMERICAN WELCOME BOUQUET

This simple red, white, and blue bouquet in a basket makes a patriotic statement—and is a fun addition to a summer event that falls around Flag Day (June 14), the Fourth of July, or another date that has personal meaning for you. The blue-and-white bandana adds color and a touch of country whimsy. This basket of blooms is a perfect arrangement for an outdoor luncheon, brunch, or barbecue. Of course, you can simply change the colors of the carnations and bandana to create a theme and color scheme of your own.

SWEET REHEARSAL DINNER CENTERPIECE

Rehearsal dinner décor and centerpieces should be casual and fun. Save the formal touches for your wedding day. This ring of flowers is made of bright orange and red ranunculus, deep purple hyacinths, and simple greenery. Glass cylinders of staggering heights are filled with assorted, colorful candies. The center cylinder contains a floating candle.

FRUIT TERRARIUM

Make your guests feel right at home with these simple, colorful terrariums. Clear glass containers with matching lids come in assorted shapes and sizes. They're perfect for housing fresh-looking faux lemons and Granny Smith apples such as these—or any other type of fruit in colors you prefer, depending on your season or theme. You can also fill the containers with colorful candies or glistening holiday ornaments. Add a color-coordinated welcome card—perhaps even in the native or ancestral language of your family or guests—printed on heavy cardstock to personalize your greeting.

GERBERA DAISY BLOCK

These bright and cheery gerbera daisy blocks add a dramatic splash of color. These hot-orange shades are great for a sunny afternoon event. Choose a pale pastel for a bridal shower or white flowers for a glamorous evening affair. Simply secure the blooms to foam cubes with hot glue. Cubes come in several sizes. You could also stack them or arrange them side by side to create a brilliant tablescape.

CHAPTER 9

PATHWAY, AISLE, AND ENTRYWAY DÉCOR

What better way to make a dramatic entrance than with colorful flower arrangements and glowing candles? Add a bit of romantic elegance to a walkway by placing a series of floating candles to guide your guests' footsteps. If the path is in a natural or wooded setting, sprinkle handfuls of rose petals, too, to mark the way. Frame a stairway with dramatic iron candelabras for a grand, illuminated entrance. For the ceremony, hang small buckets brimming with seasonal foliage at the ends of the pews to decorate the aisle with simple, elegant style.

DOORWAY DROP FESTOON

Small details can make a big impact. These flower balls are a simple but glamorous welcome to the ceremony—whether hung from an exterior iron railing, as shown here, or suspended next to doorways or on interior beams or arches. Smaller versions make an ideal decoration at the edges or corners of a chuppah, the canopy included in traditional Jewish wedding ceremonies. As you plan, consider the style of the architecture in your location, the best and most visible positions for hanging, and any floral or decorating restrictions.

Here are the materials you will need to make one doorway drop festoon:

- one 12" (30.5 cm) plastic-foam ball
- two large bunches of flowers (one each of cranberry and purple)
- 2 yd. (1.8 m) of 1/2" (1.3 cm)-wide ivory satin ribbon
- floral pin
- one roll of 2" (5 cm)-wide white satin ribbon
- floral snips
- hot-glue gun
- floral wire
- scissors

STEP 1. Cut all the blossoms off the flowers so that the stems are short, about 1"
(2.5 cm), as shown here. Press one blossom stem into the plastic-foam
ball and push down to hold it in place. Glue around the stem to secure it.
Repeat with the remaining blossoms until the entire ball is covered.

STEP 2. Loop the narrow ribbon around the flower ball four times, leaving a 16"
(40.5 cm) length of ribbon for a tail at each end. Push the floral pin
around the center of the loops and secure the ribbon to the ball.

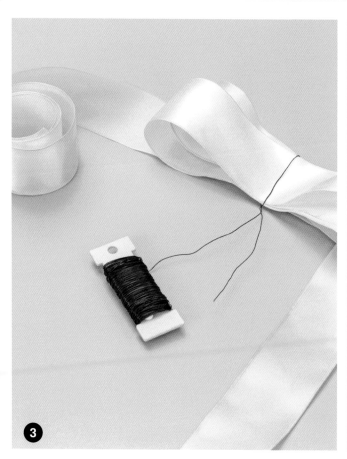

STEP 3.   To make the bow, fold the wide ribbon to make four loops, leaving a length of ribbon approximately 18" (45.5 cm) in length for a tail. Roll out the ribbon another 18" (45.5 cm) for the tail at the other end. Holding the center tightly, wrap floral wire around the ribbon and twist a few times to secure.

STEP 4.   Squeeze the wire together to make the bow bunched and full. Fluff out the loops. Cut the wire. Trim the ribbon ends straight across or at an angle, whichever you prefer.

FLORAL ARCH

Floral arches are a lovely way to embellish an entryway, whether it's the entrance to the ceremony, the reception, or any other event. By simply weaving together an array of your favorite flowers, you can create a fantastic frame for the occasion—and a gorgeous backdrop for photos! This arch has a base of green ivy, which makes it easy to fasten bunches of blue hydrangeas, ribbon-tied wheat, hops, and lilies securely. Make small arrangements with the same flowers for chair swags, napkin décor, or even the bride and groom's car.

Here are the materials you will need to make one arch:

- three 6' (1.8 m) lengths of ivy
- two large bunches of wheat (16 to 20 stems each)
- natural-colored raffia
- eight blue hydrangeas
- sixteen white lilies
- five stems of hops
- 3 yd. (2.7 m) of 1½" (4 cm)-wide sheer ribbon
- floral wire
- floral snips

STEP 1. Lay the three lengths of ivy side by side. Beginning at one end, firmly wire the strands together to form a strong, lusciously full base for the other elements.

STEP 2. Break the wheat to make small lengths. Form small bunches of six or seven stems each. Tie each bunch with a short length of raffia.

STEP 3. Cut the stems of the hydrangeas, lilies, and hops to about 3" (7.5 cm) in length. Starting at one end of the ivy base, wrap in the flowers and sheer-ribbon bows with wire, creating an attractive sequence as you go. (The sequence shown in the photo on page 24 is hydrangeas, lilies, and hops, followed by a bow with two bunches of wheat.)

STEP 4.   Continue working in sequence until you have filled in the entire length
of the floral arch.

Try this!

To make a full bow, form three loops with the sheer ribbon. Wire the
base of the loops, leaving a length of ribbon for the tail. Cut the wire
and wrap in place.

More Ideas

SWEETHEART WREATH

Love is truly in the air with this peony-covered heart, hanging in the window at the reception, on the church's front door, over the bride's and groom's seats at the dinner table, or even above the wedding cake display. Fashioned from a heart-shaped grapevine base adorned with ivy tendrils and blousy peonies, this wreath is accented with a few white lilies. Of course, all the blossoms are faux, so you can make it well ahead of the wedding day. Instead of peonies, you could also choose roses, magnolias, or another big-blossomed flower.

PAPER BAG LUMINARIAS

Candlelight instantly adds romance to any setting, especially on a warm summer evening. These simple paper bags are an ideal way to illuminate a pathway for your wedding guests. Look for colorful bags that match your décor or theme. For an easy, artistic touch, punch shapes in the top edges with a decorative hole punch—available in star, heart, or many other shapes. You'll also need a glass votive and candle for each bag. The votive will protect the flame and provide a weight for the bag.

FLORAL PEW BUCKETS

These autumnal adornments set the stage for your ceremony and decorate the wedding aisle with high style. Orange lanterns, berries, and assorted foliage make a seasonal accent for the crimson peonies and chocolate cosmos. All the stems are secured in foam. Tie small tin buckets to the pew ends with a length of cream-colored satin ribbon. When the ceremony is over, you can untie the buckets and display them at the reception.

FLOATING CANDLE PATHWAY

Gently lead your guests to the ceremony, the cocktail area, or dinner reception with these floating candles and a blanket of pretty flower petals. Each glass hurricane contains a brightly-colored blossom in its base and a single floating candle. To add a little more light, place another one or two floating candles in each hurricane. To sweeten the air, float scented candles. The petals scattered in the pathway add romance and drama—and even help mark the way, especially after night falls.

ENTRYWAY CANDELABRAS

These candelabras light the way with understated elegance that won't break your budget. You can find these simple iron frames—or others like them—at any large craft store. Wrap the frames in lengths of ivy, stephanotis, and deep-purple lisianthus blossoms. Mount the frames with white pillar candles and tall, glass candleholders that not only add to the design but also protect the flames from drafts and breezes. For more illumination, position votive candles along the steps, making sure to keep them to the side, out of the flow of traffic.

CHAPTER 10

SPECIALTY FLOWERS

Specialty flowers are those little extra details that set your wedding apart. After you've selected the flowers for your bridal bouquet, you still have lots of other flower choices to make: the bouquets for the bridesmaids and maid of honor; the flower girl's basket and barrettes; boutonnieres for the groom, groomsmen, and father of the bride; and corsages for mothers and grandmothers. All the flowers you choose should reflect the style, theme, and colors of your wedding—and coordinate with the clothing, of course—to ensure that you and your party are high on aisle style.

TWO FLOWER GIRL BARRETTES

Being a flower girl is a very big deal to a little person. The responsibility can be quite exciting and maybe even a little overwhelming. Let the little girls in your life know how much you appreciate their taking part in your special day. These sweet and simple barrettes—in two styles—are a great gift that will do just that. Your flower girl will love them long after she has proudly skipped down the aisle.

Here are the materials you will need to make one of the bunched flower barrettes:

- one small bunch of velvet appliqué flowers, about 2" (5 cm) long

- one metal barrette, about 1³/₄" (4.5 cm) long and ¹/₄" (6 mm) wide

- fabric craft glue

- approximately 6" (15 cm) of ³/₈" (1 cm)-wide grosgrain ribbon

- small paper clip

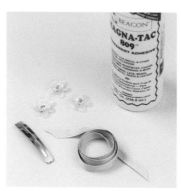

Here are the materials you will need to make one of the appliqué flower barrettes:

- approximately 2" (5 cm) of ³/₈" (1 cm)-wide grosgrain ribbon

- one metal barrette, about 2" (5 cm) long and ¹/₄" (6 mm) wide

- fabric craft glue

- three small fabric appliqué flowers, about ³/₄" (2 cm) wide (choose flowers that will sit flat)

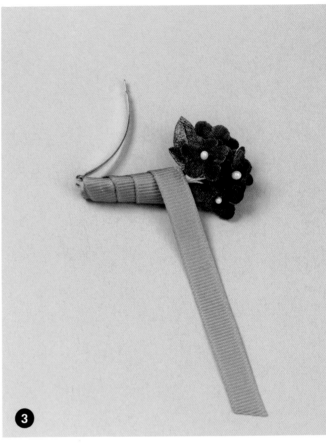

To make the bunched flower barrette:

STEP 1.   Glue the stem of the flower bunch to the top of the barrette so that the flowers are sticking out of the top. Let the glue dry completely.

STEP 2.   Secure one end of the ribbon to the bottom inside of the barrette with a small amount of glue. Let the glue dry completely.

STEP 3.   Wrap the rest of the ribbon tightly around the barrette until the entire stem is covered up to the base of the flowers. Secure the ribbon end to the inside of the barrette with a small amount of glue. Hold the ribbon in place with a small paper clip until the glue dries.

STEP 4.   Trim any ribbon that sticks out beyond the barrette.

To make the appliqué flower barrette:

STEP 1. Cut a piece of ribbon the exact length of the barrette and glue it to the top. Let the glue dry completely.

STEP 2. Glue the three flowers onto the barrette so that they are evenly spaced and the two on each end overhang the barrette end slightly. Allow the glue to dry completely.

FLOWER GIRL BASKET

As dainty as the little one carrying it, a flower girl basket should have a personality all its own. This basket is feather-light, and the handle gives little hands something to hold on to in case of stage fright!

For a winter wedding, cover the basket with deep-red anemone blossoms and wrap the handle with red velvet ribbon. For autumn, choose chrysanthemums in a rainbow of colors, paired with a bit of foliage or berries. Orchid blossoms are ideal for a tropical summer look.

Here are the materials you will need to make one flower girl basket:

- five hydrangea heads in soft green and pink tones
- one small, unfinished basket
- 1 yd. (1 m) of decorative ribbon
- hot-glue gun and glue sticks
- scissors

STEP 1. Remove all the blossoms from the hydrangeas. Cut off any traces of the plastic stems at the base of the blossoms.

STEP 2. Working with the glue gun, glue individual blossoms to the sides of the basket. Layer the blossoms so the surface of the basket is completely covered. Let the glue set.

STEP 3. Place one end of ribbon flat along the inside of one end of the handle. Hot-glue the ribbon end in place.

STEP 4.   Wrap the ribbon around the handle, holding it taut as you go. Layer the
ribbon wraps so that just the ends overlap, to create a smooth surface on
the wrapped handle. Continue wrapping until the entire handle is covered.

STEP 5.   Cut the ribbon from the spool and glue the end in place at the base of
the handle.

Try this!

Choose a type of flower that has a flat bottom so it adheres securely
to the surface of the basket.

VICTORIAN NOSEGAY

Traditionally, each flower in a Victorian nosegay had a special meaning. Roses meant love. Lilies meant devotion. A nosegay is made of rings of several types of flowers, which creates a stunning circular design. Just as it was during the late nineteenth century, today the nosegay is a truly romantic arrangement, perfect for wedding celebrations. Make nosegays for yourself and your bridesmaids. You might want to make a petite version for your flower girl, too. These sweet bouquets are charming and easy to carry.

Here are the materials you will need to make one Victorian nosegay:

- one stem of purple ranunculus
- five stems of paper whites
- twelve stems of grape hyacinths
- eight stems of lavender sweet peas
- 34" (86.5 cm) length of 2" (5 cm)-wide decorative ribbon
- floral wire
- floral snips

STEP 1.   Discard all of the flower foliage so that you are left with only stems and blossoms. Hold the stem of ranunculus and gradually add stems of paper whites to surround the central flower. Keep turning the bunch to form a neat circle.

STEP 2.   After you have added all the paper whites, wrap wire around all the stems, just under the flower heads, so that the blossoms hide the wire.

STEP 3.   Next, add the grape hyacinths, placing them slightly lower than the paper whites to create a lovely dome shape. Make sure you place the hyacinths at the same height all around to define the shape of the circle.

STEP 4.   Wrap the hyacinths with wire as you did the paper whites.

STEP 5.   Now add the sweet peas. Again, be sure to turn the arrangement so you distribute the flowers evenly. The sweet peas should be slightly lower than the hyacinths to keep the dome shape uniform.

STEP 6.   Wrap all the flowers with wire, cut the wire, and secure the end.

STEP 7.   To add the ribbon, make large loops and attach them to the trunk with wire, arranging the loops evenly.

More Ideas

BRIDE'S HAIRPIECE

Swept-up hairstyles are elegant and fashionable and quite popular among brides these days. This simple floral accent couldn't be easier to make. Choose a large blossom to match or complement the flowers in your bouquet. Attach a wide plastic comb to secure the flower to your hair. Sew or glue on a short veil of netting to finish the look perfectly. Netting is available in different patterns and colors, too. Comfortable to wear and lovely to look at, you'll want to keep this understated hairpiece on all day long.

BRIDESMAID'S FLORAL HEADBAND

This sweet and simple headband is so easy to make, you can quickly fashion one for every member of your bridal party. Simply wrap a purchased cloth or plastic hair band with a length of light-blue ribbon (or a ribbon in the color of your choice). To attach the single flower blossoms (in a color that matches the ribbon), simply glue them to the top of the band, leaving the ends partially free of blossoms so the band will lie flat against the wearer's head. Glue more blossoms to a flower girl basket, ballet slippers, or other accessories to create a complete look.

MODERN BOUTONNIERE

The boutonniere is a flower arrangement, worn on a man's lapel. The bride and groom present these flowers to the groomsmen, fathers, grandfathers, and other important men in the couple's lives. Most often, the boutonniere is made of a single flower featured in the bride's bouquet and the rest of the wedding flowers. This sleek, modern version—a crisp, white orchid blossom wired together with simple greens—is sophisticated and stylish. Orchids, a popular modern flower, are becoming more prevalent in brides' bouquets and wedding décor.

VINTAGE CORSAGE

Part of the wedding tradition is to present flowers to the mothers, grandmothers, godmothers, and special aunts of the bride and groom. Often, the flowers take the form of corsages. The colors and flowers are selected to complement the wearer's outfit. Corsages can be worn on the wrist or pinned onto a dress or handbag. These cream-colored antique garden roses, surrounded by soft waves of velvet ribbon, give this corsage an understated elegance—a perfect combination for a wedding with old-world charm.

CHAPTER 11

TABLE ACCENTS

What would a wedding celebration be without plenty of great food and beverages to entice and entertain your guests? As part of your festivities, be sure to decorate your dining tables and serving stations to set the mood. It's easy to add an extra-special touch with colorful faux floral garlands and topiaries. Candles and candle pots are perfect accessories, too. Pay particular attention to self-serve dessert buffets, champagne bars, and other places where you know your guests will linger.

SAND ART ARRANGEMENT

If you'd like a bit of modern flair, this simple arrangement is just what you're looking for. The black and white layers of sand are all about fun, and the bright yellow centers of the blossoms add a pop of color. You can buy decorative sand in a variety of colors at craft and floral supply stores. Pick a color combination that complements your wedding theme or décor. For a summer affair, add a few small seashells to the sand. If nighttime glamour is more your style, add sparkling sequins and colored gems.

Here are the materials you will need to make one sand art arrangement:

- small round glass that fits into square glass container
- block of floral foam
- 10" (25.5 cm)-wide square glass container
- two bags of craft sand (one black, one white)
- ten stems of white alliums
- scissors
- floral snips

STEP 1.   Cut the floral foam to fit into the small round glass. Push down firmly on the foam so the top is level with the top of the glass.

STEP 2.   Place the glass into the center of the square vase. Pour some of the black sand into the square vase, turning the square vase slowly as you pour to distribute the sand evenly.

STEP 3.   Tap the square glass lightly to settle the sand and even the surface so it's level.

STEP 4.   Pour in a small amount of white sand to create the next layer. Keep turning the square vase to make sure the sand is even and level.

STEP 5. Continue to pour alternating levels of black and white sand, turning as you pour, until you reach the top lip of the square vase. After pouring each layer, tap the glass lightly to even the surface.

STEP 6. Cut the allium stems to 6" (15 cm) in length.

STEP 7. Insert the allium stems into the floral foam in the round glass. Arrange them so that they conceal the space between the center glass and the square vase.

STEP 8. Bend the stems slightly to overlap the top edges of the vase. Be careful when transporting this arrangement so the layers of sand won't shift.

SUNFLOWER TOPIARY

Wine bars are an increasingly popular feature of modern wedding celebrations—and a far less expensive option than full bar service. Draw your guests close and treat the eye with this tall and elegant tabletop accessory. This autumnal arrangement is made with vibrant sunflowers that set a sunny mood. The natural moss and wood elements have an organic, woodland appeal. As an alternative, choose large blooms that match your own wedding season or décor. Select complementary colors and accessories to complete the tablescape.

Here are the materials you will need to make one sunflower topiary:

- one block of floral foam
- one 8" (20.5 cm) terra-cotta pot
- one bunch of mixed sunflowers, with twelve to fourteen blooms
- one 6" (15 cm) plastic-foam ball
- one stem of mixed fall leaves
- 8" (20.5 cm) square of moss
- small grouping of grapevines
- cluster of autumn berries
- scissors
- floral snips
- floral pins
- hot-glue gun and glue sticks

STEP 1. Cut the floral foam block to fit inside the terra-cotta pot. Hot-glue the foam in place to secure it.

STEP 2. Cut all of the leaves, blooms, and flower stems off the main stem of the sunflower bunch. You'll be left with a rugged-looking "trunk." Push the stem into the center of the foam block and hot-glue it to secure.

STEP 3. Snip all of the flower stems to 3" (7.5 cm) in length.

STEP 4. Press one sunflower blossom into the plastic-foam ball and hot-glue it to secure. Continue positioning the sunflower blooms until the ball is covered.

STEP 5. Cut the stems of the leaves so they are very short, as shown. Gently fold the leaves in half lengthwise and glue the stem and leaf bottom in between the sunflower blooms. Continue adding leaves to give the ball a full and colorful autumnal look.

STEP 6. Find a free space in the center of the plastic-foam ball. Push that section of the ball onto the stem in the pot.

STEP 7. Arrange the moss on top of the foam block in the pot. Cut or tear away any extra moss hanging over the edge.

STEP 8. Gather the grapevines and trim the ends with floral snips. Insert one set of ends into the floral foam block, close to the base of the stem. Press the ends firmly and fix in place with a floral pin. Twist the vines around to the back of the sunflower ball and adhere to the ball with a floral pin.

STEP 9. For the finishing touch, you'll need one sunflower blossom, a few leaves, and the autumn berries. Glue the leaves and berries to the moss first. Then glue the sunflower blossom on top of the leaves. Let the glue dry thoroughly.

More Ideas

DAHLIA VOTIVE

Simply set in beautiful faux dahlia blossoms, these small votive candles make bright, cheery accents for any wedding celebration. These pretty arrangements provide the perfect way to dress up cocktail tables, line a walkway, or—when arranged in a luxurious cluster—add a bold accent to the center of the table. Dahlias are a showy flower, available in a wide variety of colors, so choose any shade that suits your season, theme, or décor. Add a gently scented candle for a bit of extra interest. Try making flowery votives with large garden roses, peonies, football chrysanthemums—even small cabbages.

SWEET CANDLE POT

This soft and frilly candle pot is perfect for the tablescape of a bar or buffet table. The soft pink shades of the faux sweet peas accent the dramatic black and white of the classic toile-pattern tablecloth. Simply line a decorative urn with floral foam. Insert several stems of sweet peas—cut to the desired length—so the blooms are distributed evenly around the outer rim. Bend the stems and tendrils to create a natural, cascading look. Place the candle in a plastic candleholder and affix it to the floral foam. Firmly place the glass hurricane over the candle.

BLOOMING CANDELABRA

Together, gold and white are the essence of elegance. This S-shaped swirl base (from a home accessories store) is outlined with a length of ivy garland, secured with wire wraps. Assorted all-white faux flowers—gerberas, lilies, and stephanotis—are layered on top of the ivy for a fully in-bloom appearance. Wide white pillar candles continue the moonlight-white theme. A tall arrangement like the one shown here is perfect for tables that need some height, such as a champagne or coffee station. You can make the same stunning arrangement with a different-shaped base and with shorter pillar candles, too.

DELICATE TULLE DRAPE

Give your dessert table the sweet attention it deserves with this petal-filled tulle drape. Measure the table length and width to determine how much tulle you'll need. Add a bit extra for cutting and draping. Fold the tulle in half lengthwise and fill the fabric with faux blossoms or petals. Tie the fabric at the ends and center with decorative ribbon to create the gentle draping. Tack the ends and center to the table edge. You'll find tulle in a variety of colors and widths at most craft stores. This special touch is also perfect for gift, guestbook, or champagne-toast tables.

REGAL GARLAND ROPING

It's so easy to add those little extra touches that make all the difference. Showcase your bar table with a simple frame of garland blooms (maybe even come up with a special signature drink for your guests). These brightly colored yellow and orange marigold blossoms are simply glued onto lengths of wide satin ribbon. You can buy these inexpensive flowers in bunches. The large, blousy flower heads fill the ribbon quickly. The tablecloth is solid white with a 2 yd. (1.8 m) length of paisley fabric centered on top to create a colorful, textured underlay for the garland and the glassware.

CHAPTER 12

HANGING DÉCOR

Fill the air with bright, twinkling lights and bundles of flowers suspended in space. Hanging décor adds a special ambience to your one-of-a-kind day. Imagine how your guests will feel as they stroll beneath a flower-wrapped chandelier or gather to chat by the light of paper lanterns in a rainbow of pastels. There are many ways to add the whimsy and charm of hanging décor to any type of wedding event—sure to make any wedding event truly special and unique. These simple decorative details are easy to make and are cost effective, too. A little goes a long way.

MONOGRAM WREATH

This initial in bloom is a lovely way to proudly display the bride and groom's new shared monogram (or you can display one initial for each last name). This personalized floral makes beautiful signage for leading guests to the door of the rehearsal dinner or reception. You can hang it on a fence, doorway, or even a tree trunk with a decorative ribbon in the color of your choice. Any flower with small, compact blossoms will work well. Red, white, and rosy flowers add an especially romantic touch.

Here are the materials you will need to make one monogram wreath:

- 16" × 20" (40.5 × 51 cm) piece of poster board
- delphinium blossoms in light and dark rose tones (ten stems' worth)
- large letter template (optional)
- hot-glue gun and glue sticks
- decorative ribbon in color of your choice
- pencil
- scissors

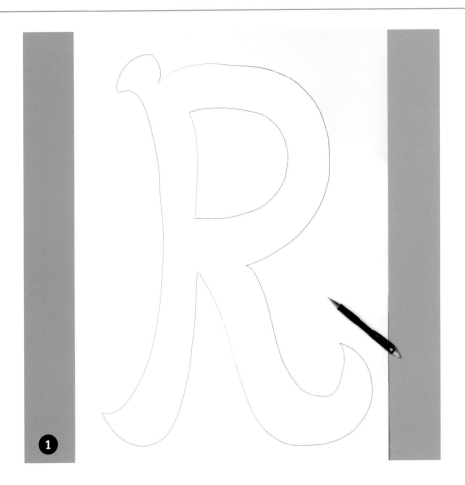

STEP 1. With the pencil, draw a large, freehand letter of the bride and groom's monogram onto poster board. (If you prefer, you can trace a template of the letter.) Choose a fancy, formal script or a simpler shape, depending on the style of the rest of your wedding décor.

STEP 2. Cut out the letter with scissors.

STEP 3.   Working with the hot-glue gun, glue the blossoms onto the surface of the letter. Arrange the flowers so the dark and light shades create a pleasing pattern. Be sure to cover the edges of the paper well. Let the glue set completely.

STEP 4.   To display the monogram wreath, loop the ribbon around the top at center. After you've attached the wreath to the perfect spot, tie the ribbon with a big showy bow.

KISSING BALL

Here's a modern twist on the Victorian-era hanging decoration known as the kissing ball. Full of colorful faux blossoms instead of the traditional evergreens, this kissing ball is accented with delicate tendrils of ivy, contrasting flowers, and a lovely wide ribbon. Start with a floral ball, found in most craft stores, and add your personal touches for a quick and easy transformation. Tie the shimmering ribbon in a bow and hang it any place you choose. Change the colors of the blossoms and ribbon to match your theme and décor.

Here are the materials you will need to make one kissing ball:

- one stem each of purple- and magenta-colored blossoms
- one craft ball covered with white roses
- one bunch of variegated ivy
- 1 1/2 yd. (1.4 m) of decorative wire-edged ribbon
- floral snips
- floral pins

STEP 1.   Snip the magenta-colored blossoms to 2" (5 cm) in length. With floral pins, secure the stems to the floral craft ball, pressing them in place firmly. Continue adding magenta blossoms until you have positioned them evenly around the ball.

STEP 2.   Cut the purple blossoms to 2" (5 cm) in length. Again, secure the stems with floral pins, pressing firmly into the ball. Work around the ball, filling in the spaces to create a nice pattern of color.

STEP 3.   Cut the ivy tendrils to 2" (5 cm) lengths. Arrange the ivy evenly around the floral ball, filling in more of the spaces between the blossoms.

STEP 4.   Leaving a tail at one end, fold the ribbon to make four loops. Leave the rest of the ribbon free to form the other tail. Gather the loops at the center with a floral pin. Press the ribbon securely into the center top of the ball. One loop is the hanging hoop. Fluff the others to form a full bow.

Try this!   Most craft stores sell simple wedding accessories in special sections or aisles. Shop for ready-made blooms and ribbons to suit your style and turn simple into sensational!

More Ideas

FLOWER-FILLED CHANDELIER

Hanging décor makes a great impact but requires very little effort and expense. This chandelier has one large and several small glass vases, which are filled with water to add a realistic touch. In each vase, a combination of fuchsia and apple blossoms are artfully arranged. This floral accent is perfect to hang in an entryway or over the dance floor. To make a stationary variation, remove the chain and place the large vase on an iron candle stand. Add a few drops of food coloring to the water for a burst of color or submerge glitter, gems, or glass marbles to add more pizzazz.

LANTERNS AND LIGHTS

Weddings are happy celebrations, so why not add some whimsy and fun to your decorations, too? This combination of colorful paper lanterns, string lights, and paper streamers instantly adds a festive air—and is sure to fit any budget. You'll find a wide variety of choices in mail-order catalogs, at craft stores, and on the Internet. The combination of colors, the number of strands, and the arrangement are all up to you—you can't go wrong. When the sun sets, the bright colors and twinkling lights will keep your party going long into the night!

COLORFUL VOTIVES

Set your wedding softly aglow with these easy-to-make twinkling lights. Simply twist lengths of wire to craft hoop frames for each glass candleholder. Fill each holder with a colored votive candle. Votives come in a variety of colors, from vibrant to pastel, and in several scents, if you'd like. You can choose one color or combine colors to suit your theme and style. These lavender and blue shades evoke an English garden. For a more traditional look, choose all white. Hang the individual votives in clusters anywhere you'd like to add interest— from the garden to the reception hall or on paths in between.

PAPER DOILY CONES

Whimsical details are often the most memorable. Hanging cones filled with small bouquets of flowers have an especially sweet look—whether they are hanging on the front door of the reception room, the end of a pew, or even on the bride-to-be's bedroom door. Roll and glue paper doilies to form the cone. Then fill them with a small mix of flowers of your choice and hang them with decorative ribbons. These delicate cones also make a lovely bouquet for your flower girl, as they are small, lightweight, and very pretty.

CHAPTER 13

SPECIAL DETAILS

Small and special details can make an extra-big impact. Carefully chosen accents and accessories add an element of surprise and delight to your wedding events—a bouquet of delicate posies in the powder room or ballet slippers adorned with sweet blossoms for your ballerina flower girl. What about dressing up your favorite pooch for the occasion with a festive collar of flowers? These decorative touches say a lot about you and your sense of style. They're also light on time required and easy to fashion—but will be sure to attract a lot of attention from family and friends.

ROMANTIC CHAIR SWAG

The soft shades of this vintage-style arrangement create a feeling of romance. Clusters of old-fashioned flowers are accented with sprigs of ivy and a bow flourish. Not only is the decoration beautiful in itself, it's functional, too. Make a swag for each end chair on the aisle to mark off the rows reserved for family and members of the ceremony. Tie long tails of satin ribbon across the aisle before your guests arrive. Then cut the ribbons as members of the family and bridal party enter to take their seats.

Here are the materials you will need to make one romantic chair swag:

- one stem of purple hydrangea
- one stem of lilac garden rose
- one stem of blue delphinium
- one stem of viburnum
- 18" (45.5 cm) length of decorative sheer purple ribbon
- four 12" (30.5 cm) lengths of ivy
- floral wire
- floral snips

STEP 1.   Gather the flowers to make a small bouquet. Cut the stems to equal length—about 6" (15 cm). Arrange the flowers so that all of the blooms are visible on one side of the bouquet. Wrap the stems together with wire.

STEP 2.   Form a bow by looping the sheer ribbon several times. Wrap the base of the loops with wire to secure them.

STEP 3.   Arrange the ivy tendrils in a crisscross pattern to form a star shape. Be sure the ends splay to create interest and to give the arrangement a wide base. Wrap the tendrils together with wire.

STEP 4.   Attach the swag to the chair with a strong, covered wire. If any wire
shows, simply make a small bow to conceal it. Or, you can tie the swag
on with a wide, strong ribbon or a decorative cord. Be sure to choose
a section of the chair that will hold the swag in place securely—for
example, through a rail or slat.

FLOWER GIRL BALLET SLIPPERS

With just a few buds and bows, you can easily turn ballet flats into adorable footwear for your flower girls. These adorable shoes are a one-of-a-kind accessory that will complement the color of the girls' dresses and the flowers in the bouquets they carry, too. Simply choose store-bought shoes in your color of choice, then glue on the small clusters of faux roses and velvet ribbons. You can find faux rosebuds and velvet ribbon in every sweet color you can imagine!

Here are the materials you will need to make one pair of ballet slippers:

- pair of ballet flats
- 1 yd. (1 m) of ³⁄₈" (1 cm)-wide velvet ribbon
- one stem of roses
- needle and thread
- hot-glue gun and glue sticks

STEP 1.   Cut the velvet ribbon in half. Fold one end over twice to form small looped petals.

STEP 2.   Remove the rosebuds from the stem. Hand-stitch several onto the ribbon to create a small cluster.

STEP 3.   After sewing on the buds, fold the other end of the ribbon to form two more petals.

STEP 4.   Hot-glue the rosebud cluster to the top of the ballet slipper, positioning it at center. Clip the ribbon ends to length if necessary. Set the slipper aside to allow the glue to dry thoroughly.

STEP 5.   Repeat the steps to make a matching rosebud cluster for the other ballet slipper.

More Ideas

CALLA LILY FISHBOWLS

Show off your sense of style with this one-of-a-kind decorative detail. The simple, modern lines and exotic blooms add a sophisticated touch to your champagne table or buffet. This dramatic and clever design is made simply by stacking three large fishbowls (very economical!). Each bowl contains three white calla lilies. The flower stems are twisted to fit the shape of the bowl, which adds to the bold graphic design. If the stems are too long or the ends are discolored, snip off the excess. Other types of flowers—tulips, lilies, and cosmos, to name a few—will work well, too.

SPARKLY CAKE TOPPER

One of the highlights of the reception is cutting the cake. Some couples display the cake during the entire reception—to whet appetites—and some simply wheel it out before it's served. Either way, guests look forward to the viewing and, of course, the eating of the cake! This cake topper is fashioned from peach-toned ranunculus blossoms. The stems are cut short and glued to a cardboard cake form. Jeweled strings, shaped and glued in between the blooms, form sparkling loops. Design your topper so it embellishes the cake but doesn't overpower it. Choose colors and flowers that mirror your theme and wedding décor.

POWDER ROOM POSIES

This pretty pairing is an unexpected and eye-catching surprise. You'll impress your guests with your attention to details, too. This vase is filled with spring lilacs, but you can choose any type of faux blossom that suits your style and décor. Purchase a tall plastic container, a short glass candleholder, and a scented or unscented votive candle. Wrap the vase and glass with wire-free ribbons in coordinating colors and patterns, overlapping the edges slightly as you wrap. Glue the ribbons in place. In no time, you'll have an easy and elegant accent that will make your guests feel special in any room.

GUESTBOOK BLOSSOMS

The small, eye-catching touches do make your wedding a one-of-a-kind affair. This petite grouping—the perfect accent for your guestbook table—will do just that. The sophisticated white lilies balance the vibrant lemon-lime ribbon and green berries in a short, simple glass vase. It's sure to make all of your guests stop to sign their names and express good wishes for the bride and groom. The best part about this arrangement is that, after the reception, you can present it as a gift to thank someone who has worked hard to help you prepare for your special day.

BEST FRIEND'S COLLAR

Here's a way to dress up your favorite pooch for the big day. Be sure the collar fits around your pet's neck comfortably—if it's irritating, he'll roll on the ground and crush the flowers. Start with a generous length of ivy vine. Snip the blossoms off stems of faux flowers and wrap each short blossom stem with floral tape, from top to bottom. Attach the blossoms to the ivy securely with wire. Make a hook closure with a short length of wire at each end of the ivy. If your dog is the sensitive type, instead make a small bouquet to secure to his everyday collar with a soft ribbon or cord so he doesn't notice quite as much. Either way, he'll steal the show!

CHAIR BACK FLORAL CLUSTERS

Decorating chair backs is an easy and inexpensive way to make a spot look pretty. Special chair backs can also designate special seating for family members, the bridal party, or the bride and groom. The gem tones in this colorful chair back express a bright, celebratory mood. The small bouquet of roses, lisianthus, viburnum, and ivy is festive and slightly formal. Centered on the chair back, this floral cluster is ideal for the bride's and groom's ceremony chairs, to be admired by guests during the ceremony. After the ceremony, move the couple's chairs to the reception room to accent the head table.

CHAPTER 14

SEASONAL TOUCHES

The four seasons offer a bounty of fresh ideas and creative inspiration for the design of your faux floral and candle accessories. If your wedding is in the spring, you might choose flowers and delicate buds in soft, pastel colors. For a summer affair, have some fun with vibrant citrus orange, lemon, and lime tones in various intensities. Autumn offers the many colors of changing foliage for inspiration. Transform your winter wedding into a wonderland of frosty whites and sparkling gem tones. When planning your events, from the engagement party to the reception, Mother Nature is a great place to start.

BUTTERFLY NAPKIN RINGS AND VOTIVES

Springtime is a lovely time for a wedding. Flowers are starting to bloom, and all of nature is coming back to life after a long winter. Capture the fresh feeling of the season with these butterfly votives and napkin rings. They are easy to make and coordinate beautifully with most floral designs. You'll find everything you need at craft or floral supply shops. When the wedding day is over, let these butterflies fly away with your guests as special keepsakes.

Here are the materials you will need to make one napkin ring and one votive:

- one small glass votive, $2^3/4$" (7 cm) tall by 2" (5 cm) wide
- one votive candle, in color of choice
- one twig ring, $3^1/2$" (9 cm) in diameter
- six to eight paper butterflies with wire stems, ranging in size from $1^1/2$" to $2^1/2$" (4 to 6.5 cm) wide
- brown paper-wrapped wire, 6" (15 cm) in length
- hot-glue gun and glue sticks

STEP 1. Place the glass votive inside the twig ring. The ring should fit snugly around the bottom of the votive.

STEP 2. Remove the stems from four butterflies of assorted colors. Hot-glue the butterflies to the twig ring.

STEP 3. Next, make the napkin holder. Attach two of the butterflies, one large and one small, to the center of the paper-wrapped wire by wrapping their stems around the wire tightly.

STEP 4.   Bend the paper-wrapped wire to form a tight letter C. If necessary,
squeeze the wire a bit tighter after you've wrapped it around the folded
napkin for a more secure fit.

Try this!

Bend the paper-wrapped wire around the glass votive to make sure
each napkin ring is the same size and shape.

FALL LEAF CYLINDER CANDLES

Autumn is rich with colors and textures. Fortunately for brides planning fall weddings, these natural elements create an instant, dramatic backdrop. Accessorize with seasonal designs of your own. These cylinder candles have the look of a first frost, warmed by the soft colors of falling faux leaves. A light coat of spray paint adds the frosty finish. Set these candles on a welcome table, bar, or buffet table. Line a pathway, brighten the reception hall, or create a tablescape by grouping them with scattered faux berries and leaves.

Here are the materials you will need to make one fall leaf cylinder candle:

- one bunch of faux fall leaves
- iron
- one glass cylinder vase
- 8" (20.5 cm) pillar candle
- ivory or white spray paint
- spray adhesive

STEP 1. Set the iron to a medium-hot setting. Press the leaves so they're completely flat. If the leaves are still bumpy, wet them slightly and press again with the iron on a high setting. Let the leaves dry thoroughly.

STEP 2. Turn the leaves so they are underside up. Spray the undersides liberally with the spray adhesive to coat well, following the manufacturer's instructions.

STEP 3. Press the leaves firmly onto the surface of the cylinder vase. Arrange the leaves around the cylinder to create a pleasing pattern. As you work, hold each leaf in place until it is affixed securely.

STEP 4. Working in a well-ventilated area, spray the leaf-covered cylinder with a light coating of the spray paint. Lightly coat the leaves, too, for a frosty effect. Let the paint dry thoroughly.

More Ideas

SPRING BRIDAL BOUQUET

When designing your bouquet, choose flowers that complement the style, theme, and season of your wedding, but also set off the style and color of your dress or gown. These classic, romantic pastels are especially well suited for a springtime wedding. Peonies, roses, lisianthus, and lavender delphiniums are woven together in a dome-shaped cluster. Pearls are a wedding tradition, and strings of the faux variety are a great alternative to ribbon, adding texture, sparkle, and elegance. The string-pearl-wrapped stems add to the luscious appeal of this full and frilly bouquet.

SUMMER BRIDAL BOUQUET

Summer is the perfect time of year to be extra colorful and vibrant. These hot-orange lilies are as sun drenched as the season itself. The possibilities for summery, tropical flowers and colors are endless. Working with seasonal florals ensures you'll find plenty of choices in floral supply and craft stores, too. Experiment by mixing in vivid citrus tones of lemon and green. Add some complementary sky-blue shades to increase the intensity. In this exotic bouquet, the colors of the red ranunculus and blue iris are repeated in the bright colors of the patterned ribbons.

SUMMERY CANDLES AND BLOOMS

Cascading flowers and bright, citrus-tone candles make this decorative trough an ideal summer arrangement. It makes a beautiful statement whether you place it indoors or out. The blousy blooms include ranunculus, bells of Ireland, viburnum, orchids, and hydrangeas. Trailing flowers, like these orchids, make a natural-flowing extension at the corners of the rectangular, textured container. Nestled among the flowers are three lime-green pillar candles. The candles are affixed securely to floral foam with plastic candleholders, which are easy to find in most craft stores.

TWO NAPKIN ACCENTS

You can easily fold a cloth napkin to create a pocket, which is the perfect place to insert a dazzling decorative floral. These two fiery blossoms—a full and bold chrysanthemum, perfect for an autumn wedding, and a sweet and delicate nasturtium, perfect for late spring or summer—are just two of the many seasonal florals you can choose from. Morning glories, jasmine, orchids, clematis, and mandevilla vines are all lovely choices. Scatter faux fruits or extra blossoms across the tabletop as an accent. Experiment with color by setting a contrasting-color napkin against a crisp, white linen tablecloth.

AUTUMN BRIDAL BOUQUET

This gorgeous autumnal bouquet is a play on rich shades, textures, shapes, and patterns. Five oversize roses are surrounded by cranberry-colored hydrangea, ranunculus, and feather accents. Gather the stems together and wire the stem tops securely. Pin one end of a wide, colored ribbon to the stem tops with a pearl-headed pin. Wrap the ribbon around the stems, working from top to bottom and overlapping the ribbon slightly as you wrap. Pin the ribbon again at bottom and trim any excess. You'll be holding your bouquet for a while, so comfort is a factor, but you'll carry this lovely ribbon-wrapped bouquet with ease and style.

WINTER BRIDAL BOUQUET

The bouquet is surely the bride's most important accessory. Choosing the flowers is a very personal matter. For example, you may want to showcase your own favorite flower type, the first flower your fiancé gave you, or flowers that you both love. In this striking bouquet, magnolias are set off by a few orchid stems, which add color and texture. The black and white striped ribbon is a bold eye-catcher, especially if the bride is wearing a white dress or gown. For a softer and more formal look, wrap the flower stems in a wide blush-toned satin ribbon instead.

INDEX